Oct. 14, 1993
Dear Charles,
Happy Birthday
and Happy Cooking!
Love, Sandy

# ENTERTAINING WITH A JAPANESE FLAVOR

WELCOME TO THE

# ENTERTAINING WITH A JAPANESE FLAVOR

by
Kiyoko Konishi with the Kitchens of Kikkoman

Kodansha International
Tokyo and New York

**Recipes in this book use the American cup measurement:**
**1 American cup=240 ml**
**1 British cup=200 ml**
**1 Japanese cup=200 ml**
**Sugar measurements are with granulated sugar.**

The author and publisher wish to thank Kikkoman Corporation for its support.

The publisher would like to thank the following for providing tableware: Flying Saucer; ginza-blume; Karakusa; Ken Green Shop, Noritake Company, Ltd.; Pavillion Christofle; Sofue Company, Suita Trading Company; Table Gallery; Washikobo; Wind Rider; Woodpecker; and Yamada Heiando Co., Ltd.

Art Direction and Set Design: Shunji Sakai
Book and Cover Design: Michio Fukushima and Masashi Miyawaki
Photography: Aritoshi Nakasato
Cover Art Flower: Sachiko Sekigai
Food Styling and Props: Naoko Shiraki
Logistical Support: Chikako Noma, Masako Wada and Naoko Yamasaki
Project Coordinator: Kawakita Corporation
Editing: Meagan Calogeras and Anne Devreux

Distributed in the United States by Kodansha International/USA Ltd., 114 Fifth Avenue, New York, New York, 10011.
Published by Kodansha International Ltd., 17-14 Otowa 1-chome, Bunkyo-ku, Tokyo 112, and Kodansha International/USA. 
Printed in Japan.

ISBN 4-7700-1451-1 (in Japan)

First edition, 1990

**Library of Congress Cataloging-in-Publication Data**
Konishi, Kiyoko.
Entertaining with a Japanese flavor / by Kiyoko Konishi and the kitchens of Kikkoman. – 1st ed.
p. cm.
Includes index.
ISBN 0-87011-951- 6

1. Cookery, Japanese. 2. Entertaining. 3. Menus.
I. Kikkoman Kabushiki Kaisha. II. Title.
TX724.5.J3K6629 1990
641.5952–dc20 90-36655
CIP

# CONTENTS

## A Picnic with a Japanese Flavor

Quail Egg and Vegetable Kebabs
Fried Chicken Japanese Style
An Assortment of Stuffed Rice Balls
Vegetable and Fruit Salad
Japanese Pancakes with Sweet Bean Paste Filling
Ginger Cookies
Fresh Strawberries

## A Springtime Buffet

Omelette Rounds with Spinach and Crab
Broccoli with Japanese–Style Aurora Sauce
Fish Escabeche Nanban
Rolled Pork with Asparagus
Tofu Salad with Sesame Dressing
Spring Snow Gelatin
Shiso Rice

## Barbecuing with a Difference

Two–way Grilled Steaks
Barbecued Spareribs with Oriental Apple Marinade
Barbecued Chicken with Soy–Mirin Marinade
Tofu Hamburgers
Seafood and Vegetables with Tri–colored Dipping Sauces: Sesame–Soy, Spicy Miso and Japanese Worcestershire
Instant Piquant Pickles
Grilled Rice Balls
Watermelon Fruit Basket

## A Cool Midsummer Brunch

Chilled Miso Soup
Yogurt Crêpes with Three Fillings
Grapefruit Salad
Carrot Sherbet

## A Touchdown TV Party

Curry–Flavored Tuna Nuggets
Diced Cucumbers with Mustard Soy Sauce
Sushi Balls and Stuffed Sushi
Pumpkin Egg Nog

## Dinner for a Crisp, Fall Evening

Eggplant Canapé
Stuffed Acorn Squash
Sautéed Tofu with Miso Toppings
Chicken Chestnut Stew
Persimmon and Chinese Cabbage Salad
Steamed Rice
Sweet Potato Pie

## A Festive Winter Dinner

Sautéed Garlic–Flavored Acorn Squash
Clear Mushroom Soup
Teriyaki Chicken
Sushi Cake
Poinsettia Salad
Carrot Cake

## Japanese Pizza by the Fire

Japanese Pizza
Green Salad with Lemon–Soy Dressing
Orange Basket Gelatin

## An East–West Soirée

Spinach Nori Rolls
Tofu Purée Soup
Fried Fish Chrysanthemum
Grilled Rare Beef
Crab and Cucumber Salad in Lemon Cups
Dinner Rolls or Steamed Rice
Pumpkin and Tofu Mousse

**A Romantic Dinner for Two**
Stuffed Belgian Endives
Tarako Spaghetti
Tomato and Daikon Canapés
Tofu Cheese Cake

**An Elegant Luncheon**
Egg Custard with Chicken and Vegetables
Mushroom and Beef Salad
Salmon Rice
Pickled Turnips Chrysanthemum
Tofu Mellow Pudding

**Japanese Fondue**
Japanese Fondue
Spinach Salad with Potato Chip Croutons and Oriental Dressing
Clear Tofu Flower Soup
Steamed Rice
Coffee and Milk Jellied Delight

**Tempura: Rising to the Challenge**
Assorted Sashimi
Tempura
Miso Soup with Deep-Fried Tofu Pouches and Wakame Spicy Eggplant Salad
Steamed Rice
Green Tea Ice Cream

**Sukiyaki: Everybody's Favorite**
Sukiyaki
Okra and Turnip Salad
Rice with Parsley
Green Tea Bavarian Cream

**Sushi Extravaganza**
Japanese-Style Chicken Soup
Hand-Wrapped Sushi
Gelatin Crystals and Fruit with Syrup

**Prepare-Ahead New Year's Brunch**
The Top Container
  Stuffed Cucumber Bamboos
  Marbled Eggs
  Grilled Prawns in the Shell
  Marinated Daikon and Carrot
  Twisted and Knotted Daikon and Carrot
The Middle Container
  Grilled Salmon with Teriyaki Sauce
  Oriental Chicken Patties
  Pinecone Squid
The Bottom Container
  Simmered Root Vegetables
  Simmered Freeze-Dried Tofu
New Year's Soup with Mochi
Sweet Chunky Bean Soup with Chestnuts

**Soba Noodles for Health and Long Life**
Soba Medley
Marine Salad with Vinegar-Ginger Dressing
Soba-Ginger Cake Roll

## Preface

As a well–known saying goes, "Food is the foundation of culture." I believe one of the best ways to understand a country is to prepare and eat its food. This lets us examine the fundamental elements of a culture, providing the kinds of insights unavailable through studies of fields like politics, economics or science. The inspiration for ***Entertaining with a Japanese Flavor*** was born from this belief, to make it possible for Westerners to learn about Japanese food by introducing Japanese dishes into any occasion for a festive meal. While the menus mainly focus on introducing typical Japanese entrées, I've adapted some recipes to appeal to the Western palate. (Undoubtedly, having taught foreigners Japanese cooking for twenty-one years has given me an advantage here.) As much as possible, I've conceived each menu around my trusty motto HELP, an acronym for healthy, easy, low in calories and preparable in advance.

This book has a number of special characteristics. One is that menus are arranged to accommodate popular seasonal celebrations or occasions for entertaining, such as "A Festive Winter Dinner" or "An East–West Soirée," to blend easily into Western lifestyles.

Ingredients that are difficult to obtain are accompanied by notes indicating possible substitutions for those readers without easy access to Oriental food shops.

Since I feel that it is important for meals to be healthy and wholesome, I've kept salt, sugar and fat content in recipes to the minimum possible. Recipes feature two to three times as much chicken as beef or pork. Seafood appears one–and–a–half times more often than chicken. And of course there is an abundance of many different kinds of vegetables.

To help beginning cooks with menu planning and serving suggestions, each recipe is marked with an appropriate symbol to indicate: "preparable in advance" ( ), "freezable" ( ), "to be served hot"( ) and "to be served chilled"( ).

Recipe directions frequently indicate ingredients to be cut *very thin* or *small*. This is because most dishes were originally intended to be eaten with chopsticks, and it's not possible to cut large pieces of meat or fish to bite–size pieces using an individual knife and fork, as in Western dishes. Further notes on serving and eating are given at the end of each recipe.

Food has been arranged with flatware or in settings that might be found in any Western home, to encourage readers to visualize these dishes for their own home-entertaining occasions. *Prepare-Ahead New Year's Brunch* is an exception, offering an unusual and enjoyable peek at traditional Japanese dishes in an authentic atmosphere.

The most challenging part of creating these menus turned out to involve the desserts, since there are relatively few traditional Japanese sweets that we can make at home. The Japanese do not customarily eat desserts at the end of their meals (except for the occasional freshly cut fruit). In this book, while subtly Oriental in name or mood, many of the desserts blend Eastern and Western ingredients, so they should appeal to any Westerner partial to his or her heritage of cakes, cookies, pies and puddings.

Although this book was written with the Western reader in mind, I hope that the many Japanese who entertain foreigners at their dinner table will also benefit, since they often are unsure of their Western guests' likes and dislikes.

I would like to gratefully acknowledge Meagan Calogeras and Leslie Pockell of the Kodansha International editorial staff without whose guidance and tireless support this book would not have existed. Deep appreciation also goes to the staff at Kikkoman Corporation, who have supported this project in every way, Noriko Kawakita, who organized and coordinated this project, the art direction of Shunji Sakai, the photography of Aritoshi Nakasato, who, as with my first cookbook, has worked to capture the beauty and appeal of these Japanese dishes, the styling done by Naoko Shiraki and finally to my husband, Kiyoharu Konishi, who had the original idea for this book, and who was always ready with indispensable advice.

If you have any comments or questions about the recipes included in this book, please write to me in care of the publisher. I would be happy to hear from you.

**Kiyoko Konishi**

Del Monte
ORANGE
JUICE

# A Picnic with a Japanese Flavor

*Portable, sturdy and plannable! Picnic lunches must be easily carried and shouldn't lose texture, shape, or their flavor, even when prepared a day ahead. Let foods cool before packing to prevent spoilage. By focusing on finger–foods and including lots of wholesome vegetables, we're ready to meander and munch.*

**Quail Egg and Vegetable Kebabs**
**Fried Chicken Japanese Style**
**An Assortment of Stuffed Rice Balls**
**Vegetable and Fruit Salad**
**Ginger Cookies**
**Japanese Pancakes with Sweet Bean Paste Filling**
**Fresh Strawberries**

## Quail Egg and Vegetable Kebabs

*Each skewer is a tempting colorful spectrum of vegetables, topped off with cherry tomatoes, if you like.*

### *Ingredients (6 servings)*

1 dozen fresh quail eggs (if fresh quail eggs are unavailable, use the canned variety and skip the first step)
12 small new potatoes
1 head broccoli
2 medium carrots
12 thin bamboo or metal skewers
salt (for seasoning)

### *Method*

1. To prevent the quail eggs from cracking when cooked, unchill by letting them sit at room temperature or by soaking them in tepid tap water for 10 minutes. First cook over low heat, then gradually increase heat, stirring water gently so that the yolk remains in the center of each egg. Boil for 1 minute, then remove from heat. Let stand 4 minutes. Drain, then soak eggs in cold water until cooled. Lightly crack the top of each egg, then peel gently in water.

2. Wash the potatoes and cook whole, until tender (10–15 min.), in boiling water containing a generous pinch of salt. Stick with a fine skewer to test for doneness. Avoid overcooking or they will break when threaded onto skewers. Drain, and remove the skins while still hot.

3. Cut the carrots in bite–size slices and cook in salted boiling water until tender (5–10 min.).

4. Cut the broccoli into bite–size pieces, and discard the stems. Cook until tender, in uncovered boiling salted water, testing for doneness (as with the potatoes) especially in order not to overcook. Drain, then cool quickly under cold running water.

5. Onto each skewer pierce, 1 piece each of potato, broccoli, carrot and quail egg. Sprinkle lightly with salt before eating.

# Fried Chicken Japanese Style

## *(Tori no kara–age)* 

*A favorite of old and young in Japan, this style of fried chicken can be prepared a day ahead, with extra strong seasoning, since it will not be served hot.*

### *Ingredients (6 servings)*

- 1¾ lbs (800 g) boned chicken thighs or chicken breasts, skin and fat removed
- 1/2 tsp salt for seasoning
- 4 Tbsps cornstarch and 3 Tbsps water for coating
- vegetable oil for deep–frying

**Marinade:**

- 2 Tbsps sake or dry white wine
- 2 Tbsps soy sauce
- 2 tsps ginger juice (grate ginger root and squeeze out juice using your fingers)

### *Method*

1. Cut chicken into 2–inch (5–cm) square pieces, then sprinkle and rub in salt with your hands to remove excess moisture. Let the pieces stand for 15 minutes, then wipe away salt and moisture with paper towel.

2. Marinate the chicken pieces in the mixture of *sake*, soy sauce and ginger juice, for 20 minutes, turning occasionally.

3. In another bowl, mix cornstarch and 3 tablespoons water, making a paste with your fingers. Coat the chicken pieces completely with the mixture.

4. In a heavy skillet, preheat the vegetable oil 1½–inch (4–cm) deep to medium–high temperature (about 340°F/170°C) until the oil begins to smoke slightly. Gently slide a small batch of chicken pieces into the hot oil. When the undersides have become lightly browned, turn over each piece, reduce heat slightly, and continue frying for about 2 more minutes. Finally, raise the heat again and continue frying for half a minute, until golden brown all over. (This cuts the oil absorption.) Drain on paper towel or wire rack. After skimming away crumbs from the oil, fry another batch in the same way.

**Note:** Deep–frying at high temperature in the beginning causes the hot oil to seal in the ingredients' protein, preventing loss of nutrients and taste. Raising the temperature in the final step facilitates quick evaporation of the oil while draining, reducing oil absorption and heightening crispiness.

# An Assortment of Stuffed Rice Balls *(Onigiri)* 

*Stuffed rice balls could almost be an entire picnic by themselves. You can use any filling except uncooked, raw foods and ingredients with a high water content. Making the balls with salt sprinkled on your hands helps them keep longer, so they can be prepared a day ahead.*

### *Ingredients (about 24 pieces)*

6 cups (1200 g) short grain rice

6⅔ cups water (1600 ml)

salt (for hands for forming rice balls)

**Fillings:**

1 egg, scrambled with a few drops of soy sauce

1 piece tarako (salted cod roe sac), grilled until pale pink and cut in 1/2–inch (1½ cm) lengths

2–3 thin slices of Japanese pickled white radish, chopped coarsely

2 Japanese pickled plums (*umeboshi*), pitted, each cut into 3 pieces

**Mixings:**

Mixed vegetables (carrots, green peas and corn, frozen) cooked in boiling water with a pinch of salt

3 tablespoons raisins, softened in lukewarm water for 5 minutes, then drained

**Wrapping:**

2–3 sheets nori (if this black seaweed is unavailable, substitute romaine lettuce or Japanese green shiso leaves)

### *Method*

**How to cook plain rice:**

1. Rinse the rice with cold tap water, gently stirring with your hands until water becomes milky–colored. Pour off water and rinse rice again, repeating 3 or 4 times until the water becomes almost clear. Soak in water (about 10% greater volume of water than rice) for 30 minutes or longer (up to overnight) in a heavy pot covered with a tight lid. The pot should have a capacity 3 times the volume of the uncooked rice. If using an automatic rice cooker, water

should reach the appropriate level indicated for the number of cups of rice used.

Note: There is a different method for making rice used with sushi.

2. Cook the rice over low heat for a few minutes, then raise heat gradually to medium–high. Let the water boil for 1–2 minutes, then reduce heat to very low, continuing to cook for 15 minutes. (Do not lift lid during cooking. If water starts to boil over, reduce heat.) Remove from heat and let stand 15 minutes to allow the rice to absorb the remaining moisture and finish cooking. Using a wet spatula, mix rice in a folding motion to make fluffy. To gather away moisture, cover the pot with a dry dish towel under the lid, until ready to serve.

*1) Wash the rice.*

*2) Reduce heat when water begins to boil.*

*3) Stir the rice to make fluffy.*

*4) Insert a dry dish towel between the pot and lid until ready to form into rice balls.*

**Rice balls:**

1. For round balls, line the inside of a tea cup with plastic wrap. With water, wet both hands, and sprinkle salt lightly over one palm. Into your palm, scoop hot rice about the size of a large lemon. Form roughly into a ball, and put it into the teacup. With your fingertip, make a hollow in the center, insert a filling, then cover it completely with rice. Close up the plastic wrap, twist tightly to compress, then unwrap. You now have a standard round rice ball. Identify the filling of each rice ball by topping with a bit of the same filling as inside, as garnish. Mixings (mixed vegetables or raisins) should be combined with rice first, then made into balls. No garnish is necessary for mixed rice balls.

**For triangular rice balls:** after taking the rice (with filling or mixing) from the teacup, form into a triangle between your palms. By holding the rice cupped in your left hand (if you are right–handed), shape rice with your cupped right hand. Gently toss and rotate to form the sides and edges as you go. For cylinder–shaped balls, use the same method as for triangles, tossing in shape between both hands. Cut nori or sliced smoked salmon in 1–inch (2½cm) wide strips and wrap around each ball, triangle or cylinder, if desired.

*1) Form into a triangle between your palms by gently tossing and rotating, forming the sides and edges as you go.*

*2) Wrap nori strips around each triangle.*

## Vegetable and Fruit Salad

*A simple, colorful salad with a nice tangy dressing.*

***Ingredients (6 servings)***

1 medium–size lettuce, torn into bite–size pieces

2 Japanese cucumbers or 1 American cucumber, sliced thin

1 each large green and yellow peppers, cored and sliced into thin rings

10 radishes, stems discarded

2 oranges, cut in thin round slices

**Dressing:**

1/3 tsp salt

3 Tbsps rice vinegar or slightly diluted cider vinegar

5 Tbsps vegetable oil

1 Tbsp soy sauce

*Method*

1. Whisk together all the dressing ingredients.

2. Combine vegetables (except for the radishes) and oranges in a large bowl. Gently toss together with enough dressing to coat all pieces lightly, then top with radishes.

## Ginger Cookies

*A Japanese–style cookie with the flavor of fresh ginger and a sprinkling of sesame.*

***Ingredients***

2½ cups (300 g) all–purpose flour

2/3 tsp baking powder

2 tsps ground ginger

2 tsps ginger juice (grate ginger root and squeeze out juice using your fingers, but if ginger root is unavailable, double the amount of ground ginger instead)

3/4 cup (150 g) butter or margarine

2/5 cup (100 g) sugar

2 eggs, beaten

pinch of salt

vanilla oil or extract

**Toppings:**

2 Tbsps sesame seeds

2 Tbsps coarsely chopped candied cherries (optional)

*Method*

1. Sift the flour, baking powder, ground ginger and salt together.

2. Cream the butter, adding sugar gradually until fluffy. Then stir in beaten eggs, ginger juice and vanilla oil or extract, blending well. Add the mixture of flour, baking powder, ginger and salt in two batches, continuing to blend until smooth. Cover and put in refrigerator for 30 minutes.

3. Spoon the mixture into a pastry bag fitted with a pastry tube. Pipe out oblong pieces, about 2 × 1–inch (5 × 2½–cm), on an ungreased cookie sheet, separating them roughly 1 inch apart. Sprinkle the tops with sesame seeds or the chopped cherries.

4. Bake in a preheated oven at 320°–340°F (160°–170°C) for 12–13 minutes, or until golden brown. Cool on a wire rack. Makes about 40.

## Japanese Pancakes with Sweet Bean Paste Filling (*Dora–yaki*)

*Often made with azuki bean paste, traditional Japanese sweets are lower in calories than Western cakes, which usually contain butter and milk or cream. You can broaden your gustatory horizons by using bean paste as a topping or filling for pancakes or crêpes.*

***Ingredients (about 10 double–layer pancakes)***

**Filling *(tsubushi–an)* to be prepared the night before:**

1¼ cups (250 g) azuki beans
1 cup (250 g) sugar
1 Tbsp honey
pinch of salt

**Pancakes:**

4 eggs, beaten well
3/4 cup (200 g) sugar
1 Tbsp honey
1 Tbsp mirin or sweet white wine
1 tsp baking soda
2/5 cup (90 ml) water plus 2 extra tsps
2 cups (240 g) all–purpose flour
vegetable oil (for greasing frying pan lightly)
extra water (to dissolve baking soda)

*Method*

**For filling:**

1. Soak azuki beans for 6–7 hours, or overnight, in volume of water 3–4 times the amount of the beans. Cook over medium heat. When water begins to boil, add 1 cup of cold water. When water boils again, drain beans in colander. Soaking, boiling and draining will remove any bitterness from the beans. Return to the pot, and add cold water 1 inch (2½ cm) higher than the beans. Cook over low heat for about 1 hour until beans have become soft. Drain again.

2. Again return beans to the pot, adding 1/3 cup of the sugar, and cook over medium heat, mixing

continuously until sugar has dissolved. Add the second 1/3, then the remaining 1/3, repeating the same mixing process. Mix in honey to make pasty. Last, add a pinch of salt. By this time the beans should be naturally mashed. The paste is ready to be used when cooled.

*1) Soak the beans in water.*

**For pancakes:**

1. Beat eggs in a bowl, then mix in sugar. Add honey and mirin, continuing to mix well. Dissolve baking soda in 2 teaspoons water, then stir into the mixture. Mix in half the water (1/5 cup or 4 tablespoons).

*2) Pour water into the pot to check boiling.*

2. Whisk into batter 1/3 of flour (sifted). After blending well, add another 1/3. Add the last 1/3 of flour in the same manner. Cover bowl with a damp dish towel and let stand for 15 minutes. Blend in the remaining water.

*3) Drain the water.*

3. Over low heat, heat a frying pan or an electric skillet, lightly greased with vegetable oil. Remove excess oil using tissue paper. With a ladle, scoop about 2½ tablespoons of batter onto the skillet, allowing the batter to spread by itself. This makes a round pancake 4 inches (10 cm) in diameter.

*4) Drain a second time.*

4. When tiny bubbles begin to form on the pancake surface, gently turn over. Cook for half a minute longer, then remove from skillet and let cool on a wire rack. Pour and cook the remaining pancake batter. To assemble, spread the bean paste filling 1/8–inch (1/2–cm) thick in the middle of a pancake, leaving the edges bare. Press a second on top, then seal the edges together with your fingers.

*5) Add 1/3 amount of the sugar.*

# A Springtime Buffet

*Springtime has arrived when asparagus and broccoli bloom on the greengrocer's shelves. Strawberries are natural confectionary perfection to sweeten warm wintry hearts. Dainty edible fish and tofu, the cheese of the earth, complete springtime's menu of bounty.*

**Omelette Rounds with Spinach and Crab**
**Broccoli with Japanese Aurora Sauce**
**Fish Escabeche Nanban**
**Rolled Pork with Asparagus**
**Tofu Salad with Sesame Dressing**
**Spring Snow Gelatin**
**Shiso Rice**

## Omelette Rounds with Spinach and Crab
(*Horenso to kani no atsu–yaki tamago*) 

*Spring brings thoughts of Easter eggs with colorfully decorated exteriors. But these omelette rounds boast an ornamented interior core of crab (or anchovies or liver paste) and spinach–upholstered with egg crêpe on the outside.*

### *Ingredients (2 rolls, 6 servings)*

6 eggs

6 oz (170 g) spinach

3½ oz (100 g) crab meat, canned or parboiled (if unavailable, substitute 3 sticks imitation crab meat)

vegetable oil (for greasing frying pan lightly)

1 Tbsp sugar

1/4 tsp salt

a few drops soy sauce

**Condiments:**

1/2 cup grated daikon (white radish), sprinkled with soy sauce

3½ oz (100 g) ginger root, pickled

**Pickling mixture for ginger root:**

1½ Tbsps sugar

4 Tbsps rice vinegar or slightly diluted cider vinegar

### *Method*

1. Rinse the spinach free of sand and soil. Submerge only the stems in lightly salted boiling water, uncovered, cooking 1 minute, before

pushing in the leafy ends. Cook 1 minute more, drain in a colander, then cool quickly under cold running water. Gently squeeze out excess water, then cut the stem tips. Divide the spinach into 2 equal bunches, alternating leaf and stalk ends to pile up an even thickness. Sprinkle each bunch with a few drops of soy sauce and let sit until ready to use.

2. Remove any translucent cartilage from the crab meat. If you are using imitation crab meat, tear each of 3 sticks in half lengthwise. Enfold crab lengthwise within each spinach bunch. These will form the cores of the two omelette rounds.

3. Beat 6 eggs, season with sugar and salt, and pour half into a separate bowl. Heat a frying pan, lightly greased with vegetable oil. From one bowl pour 1/3 of the egg mixture into the pan, spreading it thin and even. While it is still a bit runny, place one bunch of spinach and crab on one side of the egg mixture, and then roll across the pan to the other side, making sure the core is wrapped as tightly as possible. Lightly grease the pan again, even beneath the roll. Pour another 1/3 of the egg mixture into the pan, spreading it under the roll as well, then wrap the roll back to the other side of the pan. Repeat this process a third (last) time with the first bowl's remaining egg mixture. Then take the roll out of the pan and set firmly by wrapping it tightly with aluminum foil (or you can compress it with the kind of bamboo mat that is used for rolling sushi). Then make another omelette roll following the same steps. After cooling, cut the two rolls into 1/2–inch (1-1/2–cm) thick rounds. Serve at room temperature. Have guests eat the rounds topped with a little bit of the grated white radish sprinkled with soy sauce. Encourage them to try tidbits of pickled ginger on the side as a palate refreshener.

**Pickling ginger root:**
Peel ginger root and slice paper–thin along the grain. For several seconds, soak ginger slices in boiling water, then drain (heat enhances absorption of seasoning and prevents discoloring). Immediately soak in pickling mixture for 30 minutes or more. Pickled ginger is a pungent condiment for fish or meat dishes as well.

*1) Wipe off excess oil with a paper towel.*

*2) Pour 1/3 of the egg mixture into pan.*

*3) Roll the egg mixture towards yourself.*

*4) Pour another 1/3, letting it spread under the roll.*

# Broccoli with Japanese Aurora Sauce

*Broccoli is not one of springtime's flimsy flowers, but is truly a champion of vegetables. Be careful not to overcook it or the good vitamin C will be lost. The simple hues of home ingredients (ketchup, mustard and mayonnaise) depict the colors of Aurora, which means sunrise.*

***Ingredients (6 servings)***

2 large heads broccoli, broken into florets

**Japanese Aurora sauce:**

1/2 cup mayonnaise

3 Tbsps tomato ketchup

1 tsp mustard

***Method***

1. Cook the broccoli florets completely immersed in lightly salted, uncovered boiling water, until tender (3–4 min.). Drain and cool immediately under cold running water.

2. Combine all the sauce ingredients and blend well. Distribute the broccoli florets around and throughout the omelette rolls as if to frame them. Spoon the Japanese Aurora sauce onto the broccoli just before serving.

# Fish Escabeche Nanban

## (*Wakasagi no nanban–zuke*) 

*Vinegar marinade transforms the fish: the fishy odors are diminished, and the bones soften and become edible. The Japanese call dishes prepared in a red–pepper marinade as* nanban–zuke.

***Ingredients (6 servings)***

30 freshwater smelt, whole (if smelt is not available, substitute 6 fillets salmon or swordfish, 12 small horse mackerel or sardines), fresh or frozen

1–2 onions

1 medium carrot

3 small green peppers

1 lemon

vegetable oil for deep–frying

parsley or chervil (optional)

flour for coating

**Marinade:**

1½ Tbsps sugar

2/3 tsp salt

5 Tbsps soy sauce

1 cup rice vinegar or slightly diluted cider vinegar

2 dried red chili peppers

***Method***

1. Before adding red chili peppers to the marinade, cut in half and remove seeds. Mix ingredients for marinade and reserve in a container large enough to store the fish later.

2. Peel the onions and slice into thin rings. Slice the carrot, green peppers and lemon into thin rounds, setting aside half of the lemon slices for garnishing later. Add the slices to the marinade.

3. Rinse the fish, pat dry with a paper towel, and then dust lightly with wheat flour. In a heavy skillet, preheat vegetable oil 1–inch (2½–cm) deep until it begins to smoke slightly (approx. 340°F /170°C), then add the smelt, taking care not to fry too many pieces at one time. When the underside has become golden brown, turn and bring the other side to the same color. Gently shake off excess oil from the fish and while still hot, immediately soak in the marinade. Do the same with remaining fish. Fully immersed in the marinade, let stand covered 30 minutes or longer. The longer the marinating time (up to 24 hours), the tastier and tenderer the fish—including heads and bones. Halfway through the marinating process, turn over the fish to absorb the seasoning evenly. Serve topped with the marinated vegetables and remaining lemon slices. Sprinkle with parsley or chervil, if desired.

# Rolled Pork with Asparagus

## (*Buta no asupara–maki*) 

*Asparagus can assume the role of a main dish when garbed in delicately thin meat fillets: pork, beef or bacon.*

***Ingredients (6 servings)***

1½ lbs (680 g) boneless pork loin, sliced into 12 thin pieces

12 spears green asparagus

1–2 Tbsps vegetable oil for sautéing pork

flour for coating

**Marinade:**

2 Tbsps sake
2 Tbsps sugar
1/2 cup soy sauce
(2 additional Tbsps sake, for adding to marinade later)

**Condiments:**

3 slices pineapple rings, fresh or canned, cut in half
12 cherry tomatoes
mustard (optional)

*Method*

1. If the pork is not pre–sliced, chill without freezing before cutting slices 1/16–inch (2–3–mm) thick slices. For 10 minutes, soak the pork slices in the combined marinade ingredients. Turn over occasionally.

2. Peel the hard ends of the green asparagus stems, then cut in half. First place the stem halves in lightly salted, uncovered boiling water, cooking 1 minute. Then add the tips, and cook 1–2 minutes more, or until tender. Drain and cool under cold running water.

3. Drain the marinade from the pork, place on a cutting board and dust lightly with flour sprinkled from a sifter. Reserve the remaining marinade. Place 2 asparagus halves (one top and one stem) across one pork slice, then roll until completely wrapped. Secure with a toothpick. After rolling all the pork pieces, dust again lightly with a flour sifter.

4. Preheat a heavy skillet with vegetable oil, and sauté rolls over medium heat until lightly browned all over. Add the second 2 Tbsps of sake to the reserved marinade and pour over the rolls. Reduce heat to very low and continue cooking 3–4 minutes, covered, turning occasionally, until the pork is cooked through and most of the sauce has been absorbed. Remove from heat. After the rolls have cooled a bit, cut each in 2 or 3 pieces.

5. Sauté fresh pineapple slices in light vegetable oil. (Canned slices don't need to be sautéed.) Serve pork rolls with pineapple slices, cherry tomatoes and if desired, mustard.

## Tofu Salad with Sesame Dressing

*Aromatic sesame oil and garlic complement the light taste of tofu. Squeezed of excess moisture, tofu can be used in appetizers, main courses or desserts. Have fun experimenting, broadening your own repertory of tofu cookery.*

***Ingredients (6 servings)***

1 block firm tofu
3–4 leaves sunny or romaine lettuce
1 cucumber
1 orange
watercress for garnishing

**Dressing:**

4 Tbsps rice vinegar or slightly diluted cider vinegar
2 Tbsps vegetable oil

1 Tbsp sesame oil
1½ Tbsps soy sauce
1 tsp mustard
3 Tbsps ground white sesame seeds or 2 Tbsps sesame paste
2–3 shakes garlic powder
salt and pepper to taste

*Method*

1. Cut the tofu in 4 or 5 pieces crosswise, wrap in a dry dish towel, then sandwich between a cutting board and a tray, all tipped at a slight angle for about 10 minutes to drain excess moisture. Unwrap and cut the rectangular pieces into 1/2–inch (1-1/2–cm) cubes.

2. Rinse the lettuce in cold water and tear by hand into bite–size pieces. Pare the cucumber here and there, leaving some of the green skin. Cut in half lengthwise, remove any seeds, then cut thin slices diagonally.

3. Peel the orange and cut each separated section in half. Place lettuce and watercress in a salad bowl, and top with the tofu, cucumber slices and orange.

4. Mix all salad dressing ingredients and serve separately, alongside the salad.

*Sandwich tofu between a cutting board and a tray at a slight angle to drain excess moisture.*

## Spring Snow Gelatin (*Awayuki–kan*)

*Strawberries, springtime's natural candy, are combined here with non–caloric, vegetarian agar–agar gelatin to portray a bloomed, spring flower amid melting snow.*

***Ingredients (6 servings)***

1 bar (about 0.28 oz or 8 g) agar–agar (if unavailable, use 1-1/2 Tbsps unflavored gelatin)
2 cups water
3/5 cup (150 g) sugar
1 egg white
1 Tbsp lemon juice
3 strawberries as garnish (if unavailable, substitute kiwi and lemon or a fruit of your choice)

*Method*

1. By hand, break the agar–agar into small pieces (about half–a–thumb big). Soak, completely immersed in water, for 20 minutes. If you're using gelatin, follow the directions on the package, add and dissolve the sugar, then proceed to step 3.

2. Squeeze out excess water with your fingers and place in a saucepan with 2 cups of water. Heat over medium heat until the agar–agar has dissolved completely into gentle viscosity, laced only with soft lumps. Add sugar and continue cooking until sugar has also dissolved, then strain to remove lumpiness. Return the gelatinous liquid to the saucepan, and continue boiling 1–2 minutes to thicken. Remove from heat.

3. Remove stems from strawberries and cut in half lengthwise.

4. Whip egg white until stiff. Continue to beat, gradually adding the agar–agar mixture while it is still runny, followed by the lemon juice.

5. With water, moisten the inside of a mold and pour mixture, smoothing the surface with a rubber spatula. Top with strawberry slices (or a fruit of your choice). Keep in refrigerator until set (agar–agar sets at room temperature, but refrigeration speeds up the process), about 20–30 minutes. Unmold and cut in 6 pieces using a wet knife. Serve cold.

*Agar–agar is made from a sea vegetable which is cooked, strained and freeze–dried. It sets more firmly than gelatin made from animal bones. As it has no calories, it is ideal for anyone on a diet.

*1) Soak the broken agar–agar pieces in water.*

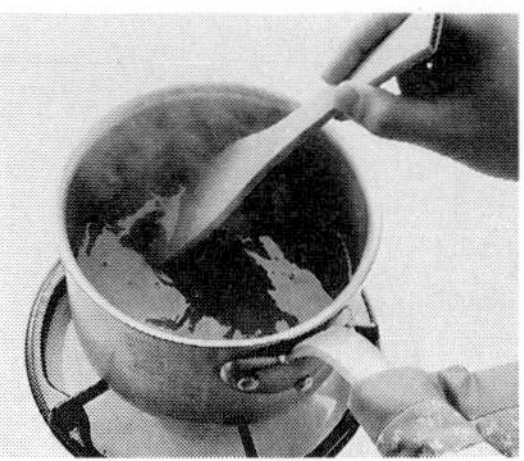

*2) Melt the agar–agar over medium heat while stirring.*

*3) Strain the mixture.*

*4) Pour agar–agar mixture into mold.*

## Shiso Rice

*Rich in vitamin A, iron and calcium, shiso leaves are a distinctive ingredient in Japanese cuisine, used often in sushi and salads and as complements to other dishes. Sprinkling them with salt before mixing into hot rice brings out their wonderful fragrance and beautiful green color.*

### *Ingredients (6 servings)*

3 cups (600 g) short grain rice
3⅓ cups (800 ml) water
1 tsp salt
15 green shiso leaves, cut into fine strips
extra salt (for sprinkling over shiso leaves)

### *Method*

1. Cook the rice in the usual way (see page 14 "How to cook plain rice").

2. Sprinkle shiso strips with a generous pinch of salt and toss lightly to separate them. Mix into hot rice just before serving.

# *Barbecuing with a Difference*

*Grilling foods over an open fire draws friends together. The secret of a lip–smacking gathering is in the marinade and dipping sauces, with pungent combinations of soy sauce, miso, ginger and sesame oil.*

**Two–way Grilled Steaks**
**Barbecued Spareribs with Oriental Apple Marinade**
**Barbecued Chicken with Soy–Mirin Marinade**
**Tofu Hamburgers**
**Seafood and Vegetables with Tri–colored Dipping Sauces**
**Instant Piquant Pickles**
**Grilled Rice Balls**
**Watermelon Fruit Basket**

For 10 or more servings

## Two–Way Grilled Steaks

*These steaks can be grilled after having marinated for several hours, or they can be grilled plain, served alongside the marinade, used as a dipping sauce.*

### Meat to be used

10 small (3 oz) boneless steaks of filet mignon, tenderloin or round, 1/2⅓–inch (1½–1–cm) thick

### Marinade:

- 1/3 cup sake
- 2/3 cup mirin
- 1/2 cup soy sauce
- 1/2 cup red wine

*Method:*
Either first marinate meat for 2–3 hours before grilling, or grill steaks and then serve entire marinade later as dipping sauce. To grill, sear each steak side over medium–hot coals, for 15–30 seconds. Continue cooking 2–3 minutes per side, depending on preference for doneness.

## Barbecued Spareribs with Oriental Apple Marinade

*A delicious marinade also compatible with many other kinds of meat.*

### Meat to be used

4½ lbs (2 kg) spareribs, separated into individual portions

### Marinade:

- 4 Tbsps ketchup
- 4 Tbsps sugar
- 1/2 cup soy sauce
- 1/2 onion, grated
- 1 apple, grated (save 2 Tbsps if you're making the Soy–Mirin Marinade)
- 2 cloves garlic, grated
- 1 Tbsp grated ginger root

*Method*
Bake in a preheated oven at 320°F (160°C) basting with marinade occasionally during first 10–12 minutes, or until half done. Remove from oven, and grill 5–7 minutes per side, basting occasionally, until glazed brown.

## Barbecued Chicken with Soy–Mirin Marinade

*Barbecued chicken with the subtle flavor of apple, mirin, soy sauce and sesame.*

### Meat to be used

2½ lbs (1,125 g) chicken thighs, breasts or drumsticks

### Marinade:

4 Tbsps soy sauce
4 Tbsps mirin
2 Tbsps sake
2 Tbsps grated apple
2 Tbsps chicken soup or chicken bouillon
1 Tbsp sugar
1 Tbsp vinegar
1 Tbsp lemon juice
1 Tbsp sesame seeds, ground

### *Method*

With a fork, pierce the chicken skin here and there to absorb the marinade more easily. Cut slits on both sides of drumstick bones so that the thickest sections will cook through more quickly. Let marinate, covered, in the refrigerator for at least 3 hours. Bake in a preheated oven at 320°F (160°C), basting with marinade occasionally during first 15 minutes, or until half done. Grill each side over medium–hot coals for about 5 minutes (away from the flame, to avoid flare–ups) or until firm to the touch and the skins have become crisp.

## Tofu Hamburgers

*The gentle hint of tofu might go undetected in this lighter tasting hamburger. Tofu and eggs (which make the meat adhere well) bring about an unusually delicious hamburger taste.*

### *Ingredients*

1¼ lb (570 g) ground beef (chuck or round)
1 block firm tofu
2 Tbsps chopped onion
3 Tbsps breadcrumbs
1 Tbsp flour
2 eggs, beaten

### Seasoning:

1 Tbsp soy sauce
1 tsp salt
1 Tbsp ketchup
a few dashes of pepper and garlic powder
vegetable oil for sautéing
10 buns (optional)

### *Method*

1. Remove excess water from tofu (See page 24 "How to drain tofu"), mash coarsely, then flavor with soy sauce. Stir in the remaining ingredients and mix well with the seasoning. Form into patties (slightly larger in diameter than the buns to allow for shrinkage) 1/3–inch (1–cm) thick.

2. Sauté hamburgers in a lightly greased frying pan over medium–high heat 3–4 minutes or until the undersides become lightly browned. Then sauté other sides in the same way. Put on the grill until heated, or 1–2 minutes per side. Eat as a fillet or in buns with lettuce and your favorite garnishes.

*Mix the tofu with the minced meat mixture.*

# Seafood and Vegetables with Tri–colored Dipping Sauces: Sesame–Soy, Spicy Miso and Japanese Worcestershire

*These mildly sweet, spicy and pungent dipping sauces can also complement sausages and other barbecued meat.*

### Seafood to be used

10 large deveined shrimp (with or without heads) with shells

10 small salmon fillets, or large fillets, cut in half

### Vegetables to be used

5–6 potatoes, parboiled whole, peeled and cut in half

1–2 sweet potatoes, sliced into 1/3–inch (1–cm) thick rounds

2–3 ears corn, cut crosswise into 2–inch (5–cm) lengths

1–2 onions, cut into 1/3–inch (1–cm) thick slices

3–4 peppers (green, red and yellow), sliced in halves or quarters, core and seeds removed

1–2 medium eggplants, cut into 1/3–inch (1–cm) thick slices

1/2 lb (225 g) acorn squash, membrane and seeds removed, cut into 1/4–inch (3/4–cm) thick slices

10 fresh brown mushroom caps

2–3 tomatoes, sliced

### Dipping sauces:

#### *Sesame–Soy Sauce*

3 Tbsps sugar

1 cup soy sauce

1 Tbsp sesame oil

2 Tbsps chopped garlic

1 Tbsp grated ginger

2 Tbsps ground sesame seeds

#### *Spicy Miso Sauce*

1/2 cup (160 g) light brown miso (nonsweet)

6 Tsps water

3 Tsps chopped green onion or regular onion

2 dried chili peppers, seeded and chopped

### *Japanese Worcestershire Sauce*

1/2 cup ketchup
1/3 cup bottled Japanese Worcestershire sauce
2 Tbsps sweet wine
2 Tbsps vinegar
2 Tbsps soy sauce
1 Tbsp chopped garlic
1/2 grated onion
1 tsp mustard
a few dashes of pepper

Mix sauce ingredients and serve alongside the grilled seafood and vegetables. Grill shrimp 2–3 minutes, until they become opaque, and grill the salmon until pale pink or opaque, 3–4 minutes per side, depending on thickness. Grill the corn for 5 minutes or until tender, turn occasionally, then move to the side of the grill until ready to be eaten. The potatoes need only be heated and lightly browned on the grill, 2–3 minutes per side. Without any preparation, grill sweet potatoes and acorn squash directly until slightly brown and tender, 5–6 minutes per side. Thread the remaining vegetables onto skewers, alternating colors, and put on the grill, turning and basting with one of the three sauces, until charred brown and tender, 3–4 minutes. Or, you might omit the basting and simply have your guests dip the grilled skewers in a sauce of their choice.

# Instant Piquant Pickles
## (*Yasai no sokuseki–zuke*)

*These pickled vegetables are a wonderful palate refreshener, between bites of those rich barbecued morsels dipped in sauce.*

### *Ingredients*

1 stalk celery, strings removed and diagonally sliced into 2 × 1–inch (5 × 2½cm) pieces
5–6 cabbage leaves, cut into bite–size pieces
1–2 cucumbers, sliced into the same size as celery pieces
1 carrot, sliced thin
1–2 each green and red peppers, seeds removed and sliced into thin rings
3–4 small turnips, cut into quarters or 8 pieces
1–2 tomatoes, sliced
1/2 lemon, sliced thin

**Pickling mixture:**

2/3 cup (160 ml) apple cider vinegar
2 Tbsps sake
1 tsp sugar
2 tsps salt
1/3 cup (80 ml) water
1 dried chili pepper, seeds removed and sliced into thin rings

### *Method*

Except for the tomato, place all ingredients in the pickling solution, covered, at room temperature, from 1–3 hours. Before serving, drain and add the sliced tomatoes.

# Grilled Rice Balls *(Yaki–onigiri)*

*A delicious addition to bread on the barbecue menu. Although called "rice balls," they are traditionally triangular when grilled.*

***Ingredients***

5 cups short grain rice

extra soy sauce (to brush on during grilling)

Cook the rice and form 10 triangular–shaped rice balls without the fillings (see page 14 "How to cook rice" and "For triangular–shaped balls..."). Grill rice balls until lightly browned all over, then brush with soy sauce. Return to the grill and sear the rice balls, releasing the aroma of lightly singed soy sauce.

# Watermelon Fruit Basket 

*A colorful mixture—delicious to gaze upon or to eat—easily modified with innovative combinations of your favorite fruits.*

***Ingredients***

1 watermelon, preferably round, roughly 8–10 lbs (3.5–4.5 kg)

1 papaya, peeled, diced with seeds removed

2–3 fresh or canned yellow peaches, diced

2 kiwis, peeled and sliced thin

1 lemon, sliced thin

1 lime, sliced thin

1/2 cup white wine

1 Tbsp lemon juice

1/2 cup ice cubes

*Method*

1. Slice a very thin portion off the bottom so that it can "sit" unsupported. Cut off the top 1/5 of the crown of the watermelon and discard. If using an oblong watermelon, cut crosswise and use half. Using a fruit knife, cut a zig–zag pattern along the outer edge of the watermelon. Scoop out the meat and dice into 1–inch (2½–cm) cubes. If you have time, remove the seeds from the cubes.

2. Mix the diced fruits in the basket, saving the lemon, kiwi and lime slices for last as a topping, and chill.

3. Mix the white wine and lemon juice along with the ice cubes. Pour over the fruit and allow the contents to sufficiently chill before serving. If you're serving immediately, add chopped ice instead of the ice cubes.

# A Cool Midsummer Brunch

*A lazy summer morning is perfect for lolling on the porch or lounging in the garden, brunching with friends. This menu will perk up even the most lackadaisical of warm–weather appetites. You can make the crêpes ahead of time and keep them in the refrigerator or freezer( along with the sherbet). This leaves just the soup, salad and crêpe fillings to prepare in the late morning. Only one of the fillings requires cooking—and one minute at that!*

**Chilled Miso Soup**
**Yogurt Crêpes with Three Fillings**
**Grapefruit Salad**
**Carrot Sherbet**

## Chilled Miso Soup *(Tsumetai miso–shiru)* 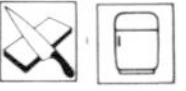

*Although usually served hot, miso soup is also excellent chilled, in warm weather. It's low in calories—unlike Western chilled soups, which often contain butter, milk or cream. Quick cooling preserves aroma and flavors of the miso soup.*

### *Ingredients (6 servings)*

- 1 zucchini
- 1/2 stalk green onion
- 5 Tbsps light brown or dark brown miso (nonsweet)
- 2 cups ice cubes
- 4 cups dashi

**Ingredients for dashi:**

- 6 cups water (makes 6 servings)
- 6–inch (15–cm) square piece of dried kelp (*konbu*)
- 1½ cups or 2 handfuls dried bonito flakes (*katsuo bushi*)

### *Method*

**How to make dashi**

With scissors, cut dried kelp in 3 or 4 pieces and soak in measured water in a saucepan for 10–15 minutes. Turn on heat and when water begins to boil, immediately remove kelp, add 1/4 cup water to stop the boiling, then add bonito flakes. Cook for 1 more minute, uncovered, then remove from heat. Allow the fish flakes to settle to the bottom of the sauce pan (5–6 minutes), then strain, either with a fine strainer or with a sieve lined with cheesecloth. Variations of this basic broth, called dashi, are used widely in soups, sauces and dressings and for simmering vegetables and seafood.

**For cold miso soup:**

1. Cut the zucchini crosswise into thin slices and finely chop the green onion.

2. Boil dashi and add zucchini. Flavor the boiling soup with miso, placed in a strainer or small sieve, and then immersed in the broth. With a spoon, stir miso until it dissolves. Bring to a boil again, add green onion, then remove from heat.

Avoid overcooking in order to preserve the full–bodied flavor of the miso.

3. Immediately add all ice cubes, then pour into a container to refrigerate until ready to serve.

## Yogurt Crêpes with Three Fillings 

*Very nutritious, the yogurt used in these crêpes creates a light, mild taste, complementing three gently seasoned fillings. Without the cloying sweetness of jam or syrup, the cottage cheese filling contrasts subtly with the other two.*

***Ingredients (approx. 7–inch [18–cm] crêpes)***

**Crêpes:**

- 3 cups (360 g) all–purpose flour
- 3 eggs
- 3 Tbsps sugar
- 1/4 tsp salt
- 2 cups plain yogurt
- 2 cups milk
- 4 Tbsps butter or margarine

*Method*

1. Sift together flour, sugar and salt in a large bowl. In another bowl, beat eggs well and stir in milk and yogurt. Into a hollow in the center of the flour mixture, pour about 1/4 of the egg mixture, blending well with a whisk until smooth. Similarly add the remaining egg mixture, continuing to blend until you have a smooth batter. Cover the bowl with plastic wrap and store in the refrigerator for 15 minutes before proceeding to step 2.

2. Melt butter in a double boiler and stir into the batter.

3. Into a heated, lightly greased frying pan, dollop about 1/2 a ladle or 2–3 tablespoons of batter, tilting the pan back and forth to spread the batter thin and even. The heat is right if the crêpe's underside becomes golden in about 1 minute. When the edges have become set and separate easily from the pan, flip the crêpe with a bamboo skewer or spatula and cook for half a minute longer, or until a pale golden brown. Wax paper inserted between stacked crêpes prevents them from sticking together.

**Fillings:**

a) Tuna and tofu

Mix the following ingredients:

- 2 cans tuna, drained and coarsely broken

- 3 Tbsps chopped onion
- 1/2 block firm tofu, moisture removed (see page 24) and coarsely mashed
- 1 Tbsp soy sauce
- 2 Tbsps mayonnaise

b) Cottage cheese and raisins

Mix the following ingredients:

- 1 cup cottage cheese
- 2–3 Tbsps raisins, soaked in lukewarm water for 10 minutes then drained
- 1 Tbsp rum for taste

c) Spinach and mushrooms with walnuts

- 1–2 bundles spinach, stems discarded, chopped into 1–inch (2½–cm) lengths
- 8–10 white mushroom caps, thinly sliced and sprinkled with lemon juice
- 2 Tbsps chopped walnuts
- 2 tsps soy sauce
- salt to taste
- vegetable oil for sautéing

Sauté spinach and mushrooms in a frying pan lightly greased with vegetable oil for 1 minute, then season with soy sauce. Mix with walnuts.

**Serving:**

Serve fillings in separate bowls alongside the crêpes. Each guest may spoon a desired filling onto a crêpe, then fold in half or in quarters.

# Grapefruit Salad

*Blanching cabbage quickly will bring out its natural sweetness. In the dressing, freshly squeezed grapefruit juice and honey balance each other.*

### *Ingredients (6 servings)*

1/2 head cabbage
2 grapefruits
5–6 stalks green asparagus
pinch of salt

**Dressing:**

2 Tbsps rice vinegar or slightly diluted cider vinegar
2 Tbsps grapefruit juice, freshly squeezed
5 Tbsps vegetable oil
2 tsps honey
1/2 tsp salt
pepper to taste

*Method*

1. With fingers tear cabbage leaves into pieces, roughly 2–inch (5–cm) square. Immerse for 1 minute in boiling water containing a pinch of salt, then immediately drain and rinse with cold water; chill in refrigerator.

2. Peel grapefruits, and cut separated segments in half.

3. Peel the hard ends of the asparagus stems, then cut asparagus in four. Place the stem pieces in lightly salted, uncovered boiling water for 1 minute. Then add the thinner top pieces. Cook until tender (about 2 minutes). Drain and cool under cold running water. Mix cabbage, grapefruit and asparagus in a serving bowl.

4. Mix the dressing ingredients together and serve separately, alongside the salad.

# Carrot Sherbet

*Everyone will be surprised that this sherbet concoction is made simply from carrots, having the pleasing color of carrots, but without their vegetable aroma.*

### *Ingredients (6 servings)*

7 oz/200 g (2 medium–sized) carrots
1⅓ cups (340 g) sugar
4 cups (960 ml) water
3 Tbsps lemon juice
2 Tbsps orange Curaçao (or other orange–flavored liqueur)

*Method*

1. Slice carrots as thin as possible, immerse in boiling water, cook for 1 minute, then drain. Repeat this process 3–4 times, each time using fresh water to boil the carrots. When carrot slices have become tender, drain and puree.

2. Heat measured amount of water to dissolve sugar, then add the carrot puree. When the mixture has cooled somewhat, add lemon juice and orange Curaçao. Pour into a metal container and freeze for 3–4 hours. When mixture has become slushy, stir with a fork to break up large crystals and to let air in. Return to the freezer. At 1–2 hour intervals, repeat this breaking–up process 3–4 more times, until firm.

Sports Pages
The New York Times

# A Touchdown TV Party

*Settling in front of the set with good friends is a perfect cozy occasion to enjoy tempting, delicious, finger–foods. Most of these dishes can be prepared the day before, so you can chat and munch with your guests, in a relaxed family–style atmosphere, around the TV.*

**Curry–Flavored Tuna Nuggets**
**Diced Cucumbers with Mustard Soy Sauce**
**Sushi Balls and Stuffed Sushi**
**Pumpkin Egg Nog**

## Curry–Flavored Tuna Nuggets 

*Kitchen fish–watchers usually observe tuna in sandwiches or as sashimi (raw fish). But tuna can also be tantalizing lightly coated in a curry seasoning, then fried, diminishing its fishy odor.*

### *Ingredients (6 servings)*

2 lbs (900 g) uncooked tuna fillets (or swordfish)
3 Tbsps soy sauce
1 Tbsp sake
2 cups flour mixed with 3 Tbsps curry powder, for coating
vegetable oil for deep–frying

**To serve:**

1 head escarole or romaine lettuce
1 lemon, cut in wedges

### *Method*

1. Cut the tuna into 1½ × 1 × 1/3–inch (4 × 2½ × 1–cm) oblong pieces and sprinkle with sake and soy sauce and let sit for 10 minutes. Drain, then dust evenly with mixture of flour and curry powder.

2. In a heavy skillet, preheat vegetable oil about 1–inch (2½–cm) deep to 340°F (170°C), or until oil begins to smoke slightly. Gently slide tuna pieces into the oil. When the underside has become lightly browned, turn over, and continue to fry until golden brown all over, for about 3 minutes in all. Drain on paper towel or wire rack. Serve hot or at room temperature with escarole or romaine lettuçe and wedges of lemon on the side. Some lemon juice squeezed over the nuggets will add a refreshing tang.

# Diced Cucumbers with Mustard Soy Sauce 

*This simple cucumber salad is awakened and enhanced by a harmonious combination of soy sauce, mustard and sesame seeds. Try mixing in bonito flakes for an added taste sensation.*

***Ingredients (6 servings)***

3 small or medium–sized cucumbers

1 tsp salt

**Pickling mixture:**

3/4 cup soy sauce

1 Tbsp mirin

2 tsps sugar

2 tsps sake

1 tsp prepared mustard

**Garnish:**

4 Tbsps toasted white sesame seeds

*Method*

1. Cut the cucumbers in half lengthwise and remove any seeds, then cut into large triangular pieces. Sprinkle with salt and let stand for 10 minutes to drain excess moisture, then rinse off salt and pat dry. This prevents the pickling mixture from becoming watery when the cucumbers are added.

2. Place cucumber pieces in the pickling mixture for 30–60 minutes, turning over occasionally. Serve garnished with sesame seeds.

# Sushi Balls and Stuffed Sushi

**How to cook sushi rice**

***Ingredients***

5 cups (1000 g) short grain rice

5¼ cups (1250 ml) water

4–inch (10–cm) square piece dried kelp (*konbu*)

3 Tbsps sake

**Seasoning for cooked sushi rice:**

3½ Tbsps sugar

1 Tbsp salt

1/2 cup (120 ml) rice vinegar or slightly diluted cider vinegar

*Method*

1. Wash the rice 3 or 4 times, and drain the opaque rinse water. In a colander, let the rice stand for 30 minutes to expand.

2. Wipe the kelp with a dish towel, but leave the white powder, which holds the flavor of the kelp. With scissors, cut into 3 pieces. Add water, kelp and sake to the rice in a heavy pot with a tight lid and a capacity 3 times the volume of the uncooked rice. Cooking sushi rice requires a volume of water only 5% greater than the volume of rice. (For ordinary rice, add 10% more water than rice.)

3. Cook the rice, covered, over low heat for a few minutes, then raise heat gradually to high. When water begins to boil, remove kelp, reduce heat to very low, and continue cooking for 15 minutes. Remove from heat and let the pot stand, covered, for 10 minutes to allow the grains to steam. Next, using a spatula, mix rice with a folding motion from the bottom up to make it fluffy. Cover and insert a dry dish towel under the lid to absorb excess moisture.

4. Heat seasoning for sushi rice until the sugar and salt have completely dissolved. Transfer rice to a large, shallow container (preferably made of wood which absorbs excess moisture from the hot rice making it less soggy and more tasty. Sprinkle the seasoning over the rice, then mix gently with a wet spatula by cutting into the rice. Be careful not to mash the rice. While mixing, cool the rice to room temperature by fanning. At this stage, quick cooling makes the rice shiny and less starchy. To prevent rice from drying out, cover with a damp dish towel until ready to serve. This is basic sushi rice.

## Sushi Balls *(Temari–zushi)*

*Ikebana (flower arranging) can almost be used to compose a platter of diverse sushi–like a flower garden in the middle of autumn. Prepare the sushi toppings a day ahead, and assemble these scrumptious "flowers" on the day of your party. You needn't make all the toppings; just try out a couple at first on your taste buds, and "branch out" from there.*

### *Ingredients (25 balls)*

2/3 of the cooked sushi rice

**Toppings:**

- 3 oz (85 g) fresh or frozen tuna piece
- 3 oz (85 g) fresh or frozen squid piece
- 3 oz (85 g) fresh or frozen scallops
- 3 oz (85 g) smoked salmon, sliced
- 3 oz (85 g) roast beef, sliced
- 2 oz (60 g) small shrimp
- 1 oz (30 g) crab meat or imitation crab meat
- 1 piece tarako (salted cod roe sac)
- 10 Japanese green shiso leaves (if unavailable, use Boston lettuce)
- 6 dried shiitake mushrooms
- 1 egg
- vegetable oil (for greasing frying pan lightly)
- extra sake, sugar and salt for additional seasoning

**Cooking broth for dried shiitake mushrooms:**

- 1½ cups soaking water from dried shiitake mushrooms
- 1½ Tbsps sugar
- 2 Tbsps soy sauce

**Garnishes:**

- 1 oz (30 g) salted salmon roe
- 1 Tbsp green peas (fresh or frozen)
- 1 Tbsp pickled capers (bottled)
- 1–2 Tbsps wasabi paste
- 1–2 Tbsps bottled horseradish
- 2–3 slices lemon, cut in quarters

**Condiment:**

pickled ginger (see page 21, "Pickling ginger root")

### *Method*

**Toppings and Garnishes:**

1. Completely immerse the dried mushrooms in lukewarm water with a pinch of sugar for 15–20 minutes, or until soft and spongy. Reserve the soaking water. Squeeze out water from mushrooms and discard stems. Add sugar and soy sauce to the soaking water and cook mushrooms for about 15 minutes, or until tender. Cut a criss–cross on top of each mushroom, if desired. Squeeze out excess liquid and use as is.

2. Beat the egg, and blend in a pinch of sugar and salt. Preheat a frying pan over medium heat and lightly grease with vegetable oil, removing excess oil with tissue paper. (This tissue paper can be used to grease the pan for the next batch.) Pour about half the egg mixture, thin and even like crêpe, into the pan. After several seconds, when the mixture is beginning to set, use a spatula to loosen the edges first, then the central section, and flip the egg crêpe over onto a cutting board. (It's not necessary to fry the other side.) Make one more crêpe. Cut each piece in quarters, and trim edges to form a circle to cap the sushi balls.

1) Drain the rice in a colander.

2) With a spatula, mix the seasoning and rice quickly, using a cutting motion.

3) Place a topping in the center of the plastic wrap.

4) Place the ball of rice over the topping and twist tightly.

3. Discard any shrimp heads, and devein by inserting a toothpick between the shell segments and pulling up gently. Cook shrimp with shells in 1 tablespoon sake and a pinch of salt, turning over frequently for even cooking, until shrimp become pinkish all over, then remove shells.

4. Slice tuna, smoked salmon and roast beef into 2–inch (5–cm) square thin pieces by cutting at a 30–degree angle. Slice squid similarly, or cut in 2 × 1/2–inch (5 × 1½–cm) strips. Horizontally slice each scallop into 3 thin portions.

5. Remove any translucent cartilage from crab meat. If using imitation crab meat, tear sticks in half lengthwise.

6. Cut both tips off tarako and cut in half crosswise. Squeeze out the tiny eggs inside using the back of the cutting knife (see Tarako Spaghetti). Add several dashes of sake to the roe and make a paste. Use salmon roe as is, being careful not to break eggs.

7. Cook green peas in lightly salted, uncovered boiling water, until tender. Rinse shiso leaves and pat dry.

**Forming sushi balls:**

Spread a 10–inch (25–cm) square piece of plastic wrap, and place a topping of your choice in the center. To prevent rice from sticking, wet your hands well (from one cup of water mixed with 1–2 tablespoons of vinegar). Place a mound of rice (the size of a table tennis ball) on the topping. Enfold by gathering the wrap together and twist tightly to compress the mound. Unwrap and crown with a garnish of your choice. The following combinations of toppings and garnishes can be helpful hints: tuna and wasabi; squid and cod roe or wasabi; smoked salmon and capers; crab and shiso leaves; shrimp and green peas; scallops and lemon slices; egg crêpe and salmon roe; roast beef and horseradish.

Compose a harmonious arrangement of all the sushi balls on a large platter, and serve with pickled ginger.

## Stuffed Sushi *(Inari–zushi)* 

*Concocted according to personal tastes, stuffed sushi can be prepared a day ahead and refrigerated. As you might imagine, this type of sushi is very popular in* obento, *Japanese box lunches.*

### *Ingredients (12–14 pieces)*

1/3 of the cooked sushi rice

2 Tbsps toasted white sesame seeds

**Wrapping:**

6–7 sheets deep–fried tofu pouches (*abura–age* or *usu–age*)
(optional) 12–14 strips prepared trefoil or gourd strips (ribbons)

**Cooking broth:**

| |
|---|
| 1 cup dashi (see page 36 "How to make dashi for bonito stock") |
| 1½ Tbsps sugar |
| 2 Tbsps soy sauce |
| 1 Tbsp mirin |

**Condiment:**

pickled ginger

*1) Douse boiling water over the deep–fried tofu pouches to remove excess oil.*

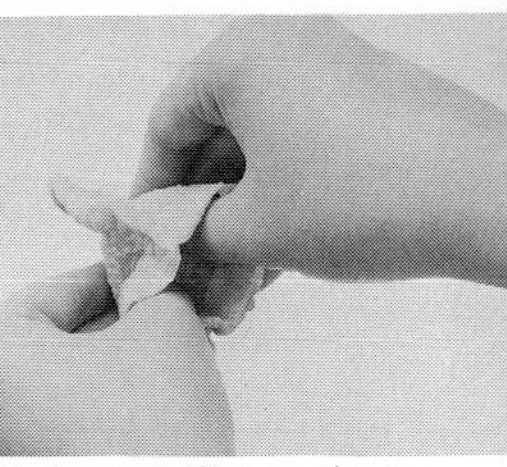

*2) Cut in half crosswise to open pouches.*

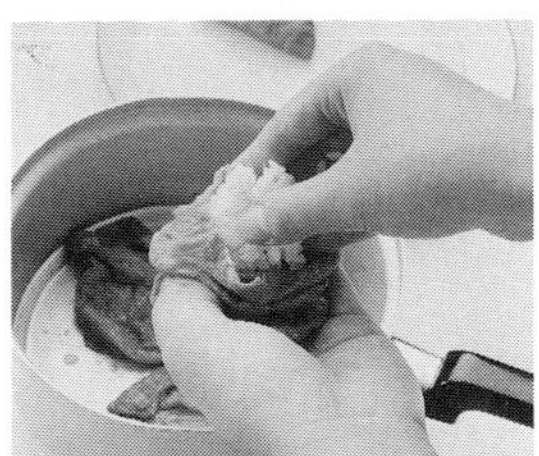

*3) Stuff the vinegared rice into the pockets.*

*Method*

1. Mix the reserved, cooked sushi rice with sesame seeds.

2. Douse both sides of tofu pouches with boiling water to remove excess oil. Cut in half crosswise and open pouches with your thumb and forefinger (made easier by rolling a chopstick or rolling pin over each piece). Mix all broth ingredients and heat until the sugar dissolves. Add the pouches and gently braise for 20–30 minutes, then remove from heat and let cool in the saucepan. Delicately squeeze out excess broth before stuffing each pocket. For variety, you might turn the pouches inside out.

Note: If you are using canned, prepared deep–fried tofu pouches, skip step 2.

3. Scoop seasoned sushi rice in the cup of your hand and fill each pouch one–third to one–half full. Fold over the open end of the pouch to form a cylinder. For a more professional look, tie the middle with a strip of prepared trefoil* or gourd strip.**

* Trefoil (*mitsuba*, a kind of Japanese watercress) should be soaked in hot water to become sufficiently malleable for tying sushi bags.

** Dried gourd ribbons (*kanpyo*), made from a type of squash, are usually used as filling for rolled sushi, or for tying rolled and stuffed preparations.

# Pumpkin Egg Nog   

*When your guests have quaffed their fill of beer, here's a delicious vegetable beverage imbued with a hidden oriental ingredient.*

***Ingredients (6–7 servings)***

| |
|---|
| 1¼ lb (570 g) pumpkin or acorn squash |
| 3 egg yolks |
| 3/5 cup (150 g) sugar |
| 4 cups (960 ml) milk |
| 2 Tbsps mirin |
| vanilla extract |

*Method*

1. Remove seeds, membrane and skin from pumpkin, and cut into bite–size pieces. Steam over high heat until tender, 7–8 minutes.

2. Puree pumpkin, egg yolks, sugar and milk together in a blender or mixer. Add the mirin and vanilla extract, and chill in the refrigerator until ready to serve. In place of mirin, you might try brandy, rum or a liqueur that suits your fancy.

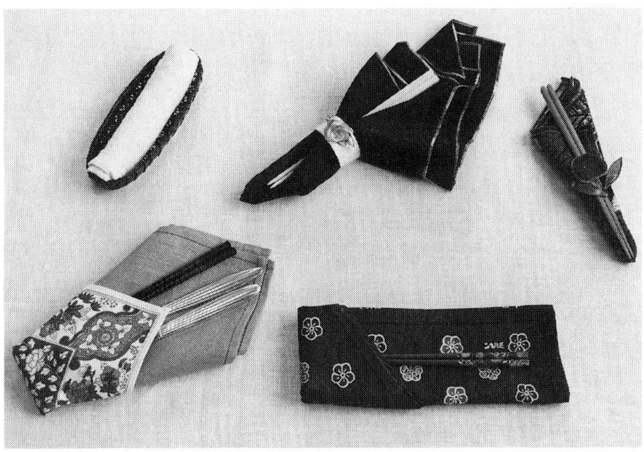

## Place Settings with Napkins

As odd as it may seem, napkins are not part of Japanese dining tradition. *Oshibori*, although not exactly like the Western napkin, is a damp hand towel, hot or chilled, used by the diner to clean the hands before the meal, or sometimes between courses, and then removed from the table. Western place settings in Japan include napkins, of course, but often knives and forks are placed on top to avoid direct contact with the table. Paper napkins are more often used as decorative elements to set off food, or as plates for traditional Japanese sweets.

Because modern Japanese meals include both Western and Japanese dishes, it is not unusual to find knives and forks as well as chopsticks at the table. This provides an opportunity for creative place settings, such as using chopstick rests or wrapping all the utensils in napkins as shown on the jacket of this book.

# *Dinner for a Crisp, Fall Evening*

*At autumn harvest time, nature's cornucopia seems most tantalizing, inviting indulgence. Your guests will savor this delightful menu focusing on acorn squash, sweet potato, chestnuts and autumn's flash of color, persimmon.*

**Eggplant Canapé**
**Stuffed Acorn Squash**
**Sautéed Tofu with Miso Toppings**
**Chicken Chestnut Stew**
**Persimmon and Chinese Cabbage Salad**
**Steamed Rice**
**Sweet Potato Pie**

## Eggplant Canapé

*Although eggplant is now available year round, it tastes best in autumn. Hard-boiled eggs, ham or cheese also make good topping. Warming the canapés a bit before serving will make them tastier.*

### *Ingredients (6 servings)*

2 or 3 large eggplants
2 Tbsps vegetable oil for sautéing
salt, for sprinkling lightly

**Toppings:**

a) Tomato and bacon:
1 tomato
2 or 3 slices bacon
1/4 green onion, 2-inch (5-cm) long
1 tsp chopped garlic
2 tsps ketchup
1 tsp soy sauce

b) Sardines in oil:
12 sardines, canned in oil
1 Tbsp chopped fresh chives
3 lemon slices, cut into quarters

c) Small shrimp and cucumbers:
3 oz (85 g) small shrimp, shelled and deveined
1/2 American or 1 Japanese cucumber, sliced thin
1 Tbsp sake
a pinch of salt

Wasabi-mayonnaise sauce:
1/4 cup mayonnaise
1 tsp soy sauce
1 tsp prepared wasabi

d) Wakame and crab:
1/10 oz (3 g) dried wakame (sea vegetable) or 1/3 oz (10 g) fresh wakame
2 or 3 sticks imitation crab meat
2 tsps toasted sesame seeds

**Dressing:**

1 Tbsp soy sauce
1 tsp rice vinegar or slightly diluted cider vinegar
a pinch of sugar

*Method*

1. Cut the eggplants in 1/2–inch (1½–cm) thick rounds, and sprinkle both sides of each round lightly with salt. Heat a frying pan holding 1 tablespoon vegetable oil, and sauté eggplant rounds until the undersides become lightly browned. Sauté the other sides, adding an additional tablespoon of vegetable oil if necessary. Divide into 4 portions.

2. Prepare toppings.

a) Dice tomato in roughly 1/2–inch (1½–cm) pieces, removing any seeds. Cut bacon in 1/2–inch (1½–cm) lengths. In frying pan, sauté bacon until crisp, add garlic, then flavor with ketchup and soy sauce. Cut green onion in fine strips lengthwise, and soak immediately in water to remove the onion smell and to keep firm. Combine tomato and bacon, and spread the mixture onto first portion of eggplant rounds. Lay green onion strips on top.

b) Place 2 sardines each on the second portion of eggplant rounds, and garnish with quartered lemon slices and chopped chives.

c) Cook shrimp in sake and salt, turning occasionally, until shrimp become pink (1–2 minutes). Arrange shrimp and cucumber slices on top of the third portion of eggplant rounds. Drizzle wasabi–mayonnaise sauce on top.

d) Soak dried wakame in water until it has expanded 7–8 times its original size and softened (about 10 minutes). If using fresh wakame, soak 5 minutes. Drain and douse with boiling water in a colander. Cut into 1/2–inch (1½–cm) lengths. Cut each stick of imitation crab meat in half crosswise, then separate with fingers into fine strips. Combine all dressing ingredients. Toss wakame and crab with dressing, then spoon onto eggplant rounds. Sprinkle with toasted sesame seeds.

## Stuffed Acorn Squash

*Filled with goodies like meat, vegetables and nuts, this dish seems to speak of fruitfulness. Acorn squash is used here, since pumpkin membrane is more coarse and fibrous, more easily ruptured when steamed. Select heavy acorn squash, as the membrane will be firmer and sweeter.*

***Ingredients (6–8 servings)***

1 acorn squash, roughly 3½–4 lbs (1½–1⅘ kg)
salt and pepper to taste
flour for dusting

**Stuffing:**

1¼ lbs (570 g) ground beef
1/2 medium onion, finely chopped
1/2 medium carrot, finely chopped
1 green pepper, seeds removed, finely chopped
1 red pepper, seeds removed, finely chopped
half–a–thumb size ginger root, finely chopped
2 cloves garlic
1/3 cup chopped walnuts
1 egg, beaten
1 Tbsp flour
1 Tbsp vegetable oil for stir–frying

**Seasoning:**

3 Tbsps soy sauce
2 Tbsps sake
1 Tbsp curry powder
1 tsp sugar
pepper to taste

**Garnish:**

8 prunes

*Method*

1. Wash the outside of the squash, cutting away any blemishes with a knife. Cut off the crown (the top 1/5) of the squash. Scoop out all seeds and membrane, then scrape inside clean with a spoon.

2. Prepare stuffing. Soak dried plums in lukewarm water until softened (15–20 minutes), then drain and set aside. Heat a frying pan with vegetable oil and stir–fry ginger and garlic for 1 minute, then add onion and carrot, continuing to stir–fry for another minute. Add ground beef, breaking up any lumps, sautéing until meat is cooked through (whitish–gray color). Add green and red peppers, then seasoning, stirring well. Remove from heat and when cooled, stir in walnuts, egg and flour, mixing well.

3. Season the inside of the squash with salt and pepper, then lightly dust with flour. Fill with stuffing, pressing gently, and garnish the top with the plums. Steam the stuffed squash (together with the cut–away crown, if you want to replace the top) over high heat until tender, 20–30 minutes. Test doneness by sticking with a fine skewer. (Instead of steaming, the squash can be baked in a preheated oven at 450°F [230°C] for 30–35 minutes.) Serve hot or warm.

## Sautéed Tofu with Miso Toppings
## *(Tofu no miso dengaku)* 

*Tofu has a humble, simple taste, amenable to myriad cooking techniques. Both made from soybean, tofu and miso mix harmoniously.*

### *Ingredients (6 servings)*

2 blocks firm tofu, excess moisture removed (see page 24),

1–2 Tbsps vegetable oil for sautéing

**Toppings:**

a) Sesame–miso paste:
2 Tbsps ground sesame seeds or sesame paste (if unavailable, use peanut butter instead)

5 Tbsps miso, preferably dark brown

2 Tbsps sugar

4 Tbsps mirin

1 Tbsp toasted sesame seeds for garnishing

b) Meat–miso paste:
7 oz (200 g) ground chicken or pork

1 tsp grated ginger root

1 tsp grated garlic

4 Tbsps light brown miso

2 Tbsps sugar

2 Tbsps sake

2 Tbsps soy sauce

1/3 cup water

1 tsp vegetable oil for sautéing

1 Tbsp chopped green onion (green part only) for garnishing

c) Lemon–miso paste:
grated rind from half a lemon

lemon juice from half a lemon

5 Tbsps miso

3 Tbsps sugar

2 Tbsps sake

1 additional tsp lemon rind, chopped fine, for garnishing

*Method*

1. Prepare toppings first.

a) Sesame–miso paste: in a pan, mix miso, sugar and mirin thoroughly, and heat over low heat until the alcohol evaporates from the mirin (1–2 minutes). Remove from heat and mix in ground sesame seeds or sesame paste.

b) Meat–miso paste: over medium heat in a frying pan, sauté ginger and garlic in vegetable oil for half a minute. Add ground meat and, breaking any lumps, cook until whitish–gray. Combine remaining seasoning ingredients and stir mixture in, cooking until consistency becomes a paste (2 minutes).

c) Lemon–miso paste: heat miso, sugar and sake in a pot until the alcohol evaporates from the sake (1–2 minutes). Remove from heat and when cool, mix in lemon juice and grated lemon rind.

2. Slice the tofu crosswise in 1/2–inch (1½–cm) thick pieces after removing excess moisture. Preheat a frying pan, and then add 1 tablespoon of vegetable oil to prevent tofu slices from sticking to the pan. Sauté tofu until the undersides become a toasted, light brown. Sauté other sides, adding another tablespoon of oil to the pan. Let

1) Mix miso paste ingredients with a wooden spoon or spatula.

2) Spread the paste over warm tofu.

first finished slices stay warm in an oven, until all the rest of the slices have been sautéed.

3. Spread the toppings on warm tofu slices and serve each variety with its appropriate garnish listed in the topping ingredients.

# Chicken Chestnut Stew

## *(Tori to kuri no nimono)*   

*Because nuts cannot be grown in a greenhouse, the chestnut is an undeniably authentic sign of autumn. Simmered with chicken, chestnuts sweeten this stew with a wonderful mellowness.*

***Ingredients (6–7 servings)***

2¼ lbs (1 kg) chicken thighs and/or breasts with bones, cut into roughly 2–inch (5–cm) squares (have your butcher cut them, or select boneless pieces)

1/2 lb (225 g) peeled raw chestnuts, or 3/4 lb (340 g) cooked, bottled chestnuts (If neither type is available, use 1¼ lbs [570 g] raw chestnuts in shells, and remove shells with a knife. To facilitate shelling, soak in water overnight, then boil for 3–4 minutes.)

2 or 3 medium carrots, cut crosswise into 2–inch lengths

7 oz (200 g) green beans, strings removed

half–a–thumb size ginger root, sliced thin

1 clove garlic, sliced thin

a pinch of salt (for cooking green beans)

2 Tbsps soy sauce for seasoning chicken

2 Tbsps sake for seasoning chicken

1 Tbsp vegetable oil for sautéing

**Broth:**

2 cups chicken stock (or 2 cups water and 2 chicken bouillon cubes)

2 Tbsps sugar

2 Tbsps sake

4 Tbsps soy sauce

2 Tbsps mirin

***Method***

1. Season chicken pieces with the soy sauce and sake for 15–20 minutes, covered, in the refrigerator.

2. Stir–fry ginger and garlic in a frying pan greased with vegetable oil for half a minute, then add chicken pieces, cooking until lightly browned on all sides. Add carrots and uncooked chestnuts and stir–fry for 2 more minutes. Add

broth and cook over medium heat, stirring ingredients 3–4 times, until tender and well flavored (20–25 minutes). If using cooked, unflavored chestnuts, add them during the final 10–15 minutes of cooking. (If cooked and flavored, add during the final 5 minutes.)

3. While cooking chicken, boil green beans in water with a pinch of salt until tender (2–3 minutes), drain, then rinse under cold running water. Cut green beans into 2–3 pieces and add to stew during the final 1–2 minutes of cooking. Serve hot.

## Persimmon and Chinese Cabbage Salad

*Like Chicken Chestnut Stew, this dish can be prepared right only in autumn. Persimmon contrasts with Chinese cabbage in an alluring combination of texture and flavor.*

### *Ingredients (6–7 servings)*

- 3–4 Chinese cabbage leaves
- 1 or 2 persimmons
- 1 tsp salt, to be rinsed off after softening cabbage leaves
- 1 Tbsp fine strips lemon rind for garnishing

**Dressing:**

- 1 Tbsp sugar
- 2 Tbsps rice vinegar or slightly diluted cider vinegar
- 2/3 tsp salt
- 4 Tbsps ground sesame seeds (if unavailable, crack toasted sesame seeds in a plastic bag by pounding with a rolling pin)

*Method*

1. Separate the thick, white sections of the Chinese cabbage leaves from the thin, leafy sections. Cut the thick sections into oblong pieces (2 × 1/2–inch [5 × 1½–cm]), and cut the leafy sections in the same lengths but 3 times as wide. Mix in the salt to coat and soften the leaves for 10 minutes, then rinse off salt and press leaves tightly to squeeze out excess moisture.

2. Peel persimmon and cut into the same size as the thick, white cabbage sections, removing any seeds. Mix with Chinese cabbage. Just before serving, mix dressing ingredients and toss together. Garnish with lemon rind strips.

## Sweet Potato Pie

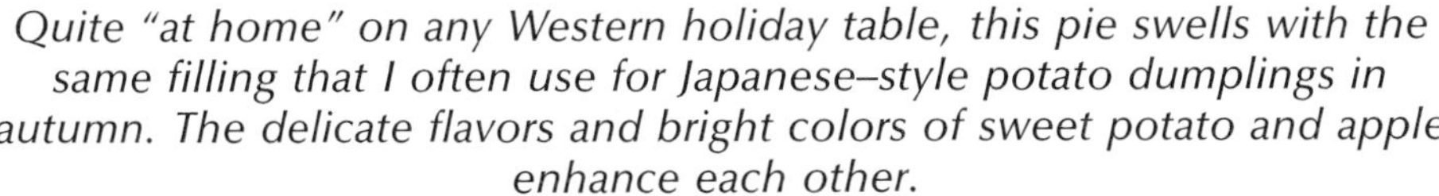

*Quite "at home" on any Western holiday table, this pie swells with the same filling that I often use for Japanese–style potato dumplings in autumn. The delicate flavors and bright colors of sweet potato and apple enhance each other.*

### *Ingredients (makes one 9–inch pie with lattice top)*

- one 9–inch pie shell
- extra pastry for lattice top

**Filling:**

- 2 medium sweet potatoes (1½ lbs / 680 g)
- 4 Tbsps (64 g) sugar
- 2 Tbsps (26 g) butter or margarine

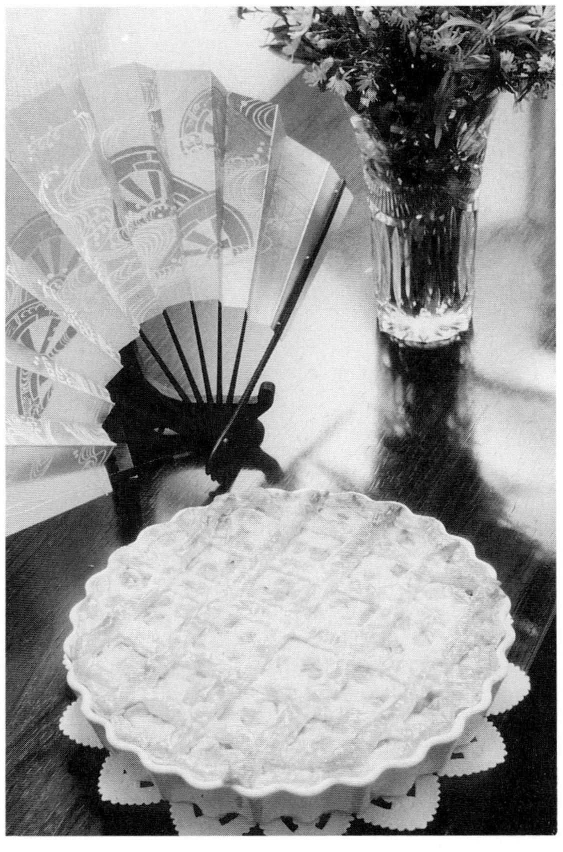

2 egg yolks, beaten
1/4 cup (60 g) fresh cream
1/5 tsp cinnamon powder
2 Tbsps brandy
1 apple, unpeeled, cored and diced into tiny pieces
1 Tbsp additional sugar, to cook apple
2 slices lemon

*Method*

1. Peel the sweet potatoes, completely cut away any dark blemishes, then cut into 1/2–inch (1½–cm) thick rounds. In water, immediately soak away any bitterness (20–30 minutes), changing the soaking water 3 or 4 times until it remains clear. Boil in water until tender (10–15 minutes), then drain. While still hot, mash until smooth, then add sugar and butter. When almost cool, add the egg yolks, cream, cinnamon powder and brandy, then blend well.

2. Cook diced apple with sugar and lemon slices in a pan over low heat until tender, for 3–4 minutes. Avoid overcooking, causing apple to mush. Reserve 1 tablespoon of the cooked diced apple for garnishing pie. Combine the rest with mashed sweet potatoes.

3. Preheat an oven 400°–440°F (200°–220°C). Fill pie shell with the mixture of mashed sweet potatoes and apple. Glaze the rim by brushing with mixture of beaten egg yolk and water to give a shiny, golden look.

4. Cut extra pastry into ten 1/2–inch (1½–cm) wide strips (a pastry wheel gives an attractive edge) that are long enough to cover the top in a lattice pattern. Parallel to each other (roughly 1 inch apart), lay 5 strips across, moistening the edges of the crust for adherence. Perpendicular to and on top of these strips, lay 5 more, to form the pastry lattice. Brush the pastry strips with egg yolk. Place the reserved diced apple where the filling is exposed between strips.

5. Bake in oven for 15 minutes, then reduce heat to 320°–340°F (160°–170°C) and bake 15–20 minutes more.

*1) Soak sweet potato slices in water to remove bitterness.*

*2) Boil in water until tender. Mash.*

*3) Combine with cooked, diced apples.*

# A Festive Winter Dinner

*Strengthening the body with warmth, and bolstering our fortitude with nutritious energy, this festive dinner partakes from an old Japanese custom of eating pumpkin on the winter solstice.*

**Sautéed Garlic–Flavored Acorn Squash**
**Clear Mushroom Soup**
**Teriyaki Chicken**
**Sushi Cake**
**Poinsettia Salad**
**Carrot Cake**

## Sautéed Garlic–Flavored Acorn Squash 

*By sautéing the acorn squash in vegetable oil, the abundant, fat–soluble vitamin A is readily absorbed, enlivened with spicy garlic.*

***Ingredients (6 servings)***

- one 1½ lb (680 g) acorn squash
- 2 cloves garlic, chopped fine
- 2 or 3 green onions (green parts only), chopped fine
- 1 Tbsp vegetable oil
- 1 Tbsp butter or margarine
- 1 Tbsp soy sauce
- a generous pinch of salt

*Method*

1. Cut the acorn squash in half. Scoop out and discard all seeds and membrane, then scrape the insides smooth with a spoon. Cut the squash into 1/2–inch (1½–cm) thick slices.

2. Sprinkle salt onto squash slices, then steam for 6–7 minutes, or until tender but firm. (Do not oversteam.)

3. Thoroughly heat a frying pan and add vegetable oil combined with either butter or margarine. For a few seconds, sauté garlic, and then add soy sauce. Sauté squash slices gently, tilting the pan occasionally to avoid mashing them. When the slices have become evenly coated with the garlic and soy sauce, sprinkle chopped green onions and mix delicately. Serve hot or at room temperature.

# Clear Mushroom Soup *(Kinoko no suimono)* 

*Available throughout the year, mushrooms taste even more delicious in season, in autumn and winter. This aromatic, delicate soup celebrates three different kinds of mushrooms.*

***Ingredients (6 servings)***

1/4 lb (110 g) daikon (white radish) or turnip
6 fresh shiitake mushrooms, stems removed
6 fresh white mushrooms, stems removed
6 stalks trefoil (*mitsuba*) or 2 stalks watercress
1 package enokidake (snowpuff) mushrooms, optional

**Broth:**

6 cups dashi (bonito stock, see page 14 "How to make dashi")
1½ tsps salt
1½ tsps soy sauce

*Method*

1. Pare the daikon or turnip, cut into halves or quarters lengthwise, then slice each piece thin crosswise.

2. Slice shiitake and white mushrooms into string-like strips. If using enokidake mushrooms, cut 1 inch (2½ cm) off the bottom of the stems, then cut in half crosswise. Cut trefoil into 1-inch (2½-cm) lengths. (For watercress, use only the leafy sections.)

3. Cook slices of daikon (or turnip) in broth for 2–3 minutes, then add shiitake and white mushrooms. Cook for another 1 minute, then add the enokidake mushrooms. Remove from heat immediately. Serve soup hot garnished with trefoil or watercress.

# *Teriyaki* Chicken *(Tori no teriyaki)* 

*Now a popular style of cooking outside of Japan, teriyaki is often used for meat and fish as well as for chicken—served hot or cold. "Teri" means shine or glaze, produced by mirin in the cooking process. "Yaki" means to grill or sauté.*

***Ingredients (6 servings)***

2 lbs (900 g) chicken parts, preferably thighs
1/2 tsp salt for seasoning
1 Tbsp vegetable oil for sautéing

**Teriyaki sauce:**

1 Tbsp sugar
2 Tbsps sake or dry white wine
1 Tbsp mirin or sweet white wine
6 Tbsps soy sauce

**Condiments:**

2–3 heads broccoli
1 head cauliflower
1 package (10 oz/280 g) cherry tomatoes (or 3 or 4 ordinary tomatoes)
1 medium carrot
3 Tbsps raisins
2 tsps vinegar and a pinch of salt, for boiling water

**Dressing:**

3 Tbsps apple cider vinegar
4 Tbsps vegetable oil
1 Tbsp lemon juice
2 tsps honey
1/2 tsp salt
a few dashes pepper

*Method*

1. Remove excess skin and fat from the chicken parts, and with a fork pierce sides randomly to facilitate full absorption of the seasoning. Sprinkle chicken parts with the 1/2 teaspoon salt and rub in with your hands. Let stand for 15 minutes, then with a kitchen towel, blot off any moisture accumulated on the chicken.

2. Mix the ingredients for the teriyaki sauce and set aside. Grease a well–heated frying pan with vegetable oil. Add chicken pieces, skin side down, and sauté over medium–high heat for 2–3 minutes until the undersides become lightly browned. Turn over and sauté the other sides. Reduce heat to medium–low. Add the teriyaki sauce, continuing to sauté, covered, turning occasionally until piercing the thickest section of meat with a skewer produces a clear juice.

3. With a generous pinch of salt, heat enough water to almost immerse the broccoli. Place in boiling water, head up, for 2–3 minutes, then turn over to fully immerse and cook, head down, for 2–3 minutes more, or until tender but firm. Drain and cool quickly under cold running water to retain the broccoli's fresh green color. Cut into florets.

4. In salted boiling water with the vinegar, cook cauliflower in the same way. (The vinegar prevents the cauliflower from discoloring.) Drain and cut into florets.

5. Pare the carrot and with a peeler scrape into paper–thin, ribbon–like slices. If you have time, tenderize by sprinkling the carrot slices lightly with salt, letting sit for 5 minutes, then rinsing. Soak raisins in tepid water for 10 minutes, then drain and toss with carrot slices.

6. Arrange vegetables around the chicken served in the center of a large platter. Whisk dressing ingredients together for the vegetables and serve alongside.

# Sushi Cake 

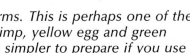

*Sushi comes in many combinations and forms. This is perhaps one of the latest variations. The colors of pink shrimp, yellow egg and green cucumber make a panoply of color—even simpler to prepare if you use smoked salmon instead of shrimp.*

***Ingredients for one 8–inch (20–cm) cake: about 8 servings***

**Sushi rice:**

3 cups (600 g) short grain rice
3 cups plus 3 Tbsps (760 ml) water
3–inch (7½–cm) square piece dried kelp (*konbu*)
2 Tbsps sake

**Seasoning for cooked sushi rice:**

2 Tbsps sugar
2 tsps salt
5 Tbsps (75 ml) rice vinegar or slightly diluted cider vinegar

**Toppings:**

a) Shrimp
8 large deveined shrimp, still with shells but heads removed
3 Tbsps water
2 Tbsps sake
a pinch of salt

1 tsp sugar

1 Tbsp rice vinegar, or slightly diluted cider vinegar

b) Japanese–style, fine scrambled eggs
3 eggs

1 tsp sugar

a pinch of salt

c) Cucumber
1 cucumber

**Layering and garnish:**

1–2 tsps prepared wasabi

1½ sheets nori (dried seaweed sheet)

1 Tbsp pickled ginger (see page 21 "How to pickle ginger")

8 shiso leaves

*Method*

1. Prepare the sushi rice (see page 41 "How to cook sushi rice").

2. For the shrimp topping, insert a fine skewer into each shrimp, from head to tail (on the stomach side), to prevent curling when cooked. Cook shrimp until pink in boiling measured water with sake and pinch of salt, turning frequently. Remove from heat and let cool slightly

*1) Arrange toppings at the bottom of the cake pan.*

*2) Fill cake pan with vinegared rice, placing a sheet of nori in between as a layer.*

*3) Press the rice.*

*4) Trim excess nori.*

*5) Cut cake into wedges with a wet knife.*

before removing skewers and the shells. Cut open on the stomach side to form a butterfly shape. Soak in vinegar combined with the sugar for 10 minutes or more to season.

3. For the scrambled egg topping, mix eggs well with the sugar and pinch of salt in a small saucepan. Cook over medium–low heat, stirring the eggs quickly with chopsticks or a wooden fork. As eggs begin to cook, continuously scrape bottom and sides of pan, removing from heat, if necessary, to avoid large curds. Stop cooking while scrambled eggs are still moist and fluffy, to lie better on top of sushi rice.

4. After removing skin, peel eight 1–inch (1½–cm) wide, thin strips of cucumber (just as long as the size of the radius of the cake pan).

5. Spread plastic wrap about 16–inches (40–cm) square inside of the cake pan. Let the excess wrap drape over the sides of the pan. (This will help later when pulling the upside–down sushi cake out of the pan.)

6. On the plastic, at the bottom of the cake pan, arrange shrimp (inside of butterfly shape up), cucumber strips and eggs, alternately like spokes of a wheel. Spread an extremely thin layer of wasabi over the shrimp and cucumber (remember, a little wasabi goes a long way). Evenly press half the amount of the sushi rice onto the toppings, especially pressing into the edges of the pan. Place the sheet of nori next, then cover with the remaining sushi rice, pressing tightly to flatten the surface. Unmold by pulling the wrap up gently, then place right side up on a platter. Trim any excess nori with scissors. For a nice touch, garnish the center of the top of the cake with pickled ginger, and arrange shiso leaves around the bottom, on the platter. With a wet knife, cut into wedges at the table.

# Poinsettia Salad

*A salad as Christmasy as any flower centerpiece.*

### *Ingredients (6 servings)*

- 1 lb (450 g) potatoes
- 7 oz (200 g) Chinese cellophane noodles
- 1 red apple
- 1 head romaine lettuce
- salt, to add to water for boiling potatoes and soaking apples

**To mix with potatoes:**

- 2 Tbsps chopped onions
- 1/4 lb (110 g) canned flaked tuna, broken into pieces
- 2 Tbsps mayonnaise
- 1 tsp vinegar
- 2 tsps vegetable oil
- salt and pepper to taste

**Dressing:**

- 1/2 cup vinegar
- 1 Tbsp soy sauce
- 1 Tbsp sugar
- 1 tsp sesame oil
- 1/2 tsp salt

*Method*

1. Unpared, cook the potatoes in boiling water with 1/2 teaspoon salt until tender. Pare potatoes while still hot, then cut into bite–size oblong pieces. Mix with onions and tuna. Then without crushing the potatoes, blend well with mayonnaise, vinegar, vegetable oil, and salt and pepper to taste.

2. In boiling water, cook the cellophane noodles for 3–4 minutes, or until tender. Drain in a colander, then rinse under cold running water. Cut into roughly 3–inch (7½–cm) lengths, or edible size.

3. Core the apple and cut into 8 pieces. Peel halfway. Soak a minute in lightly salted water to prevent discoloration.

4 . Arrange romaine lettuce leaves around the inside of a serving bowl, and place potato mixture in the center. Surround mixture with cellophane noodles. Top with apple slices with red skins up. Mix all salad dressing ingredients and serve separately, alongside the salad.

# Carrot Cake 

*A scrumptious version of this healthful cake—without the usual heavy icing!*

### *Ingredients for one 8–inch (20–cm) cake*

1½ cups (180 g) all–purpose flour
1½ tsps baking powder
2 medium (7 oz / 200 g) carrots
7½ Tbsps (100 g) butter or margarine
3/4 cup (200 g) sugar
4 eggs
2½ oz (70 g) almond powder
3 Tbsps (45 g) extra sugar for meringue
1 Tbsp lemon juice
grated rind from one whole lemon
extra butter or margarine for greasing cake pan

**Garnishes:**

1 medium carrot
1 stalk parsley
confectioners' sugar as frosting

*Method*

1. Preheat the oven to 340°F (170°C). Grease the inside of the cake pan with butter or margarine.

2. Sift together the flour and baking powder.

3. Pare and finely grate the carrots.

4. Cream butter in a bowl, add the sugar, and mix well. Separate the eggs, keeping yolks and whites. Add the yolks, one by one, to the mixture of butter and sugar, continuing to mix. Fold in the grated carrots, almond powder, lemon rind and lemon juice.

5. In another bowl, whip egg whites until almost stiff, then add separately measured sugar, a tablespoon at a time. Continue to whip until the whites form soft peaks. Gradually add this meringue to the butter mixture. Finally, gradually fold in mixture of flour and baking powder.

6. Bake for 10 minutes in oven, then reduce heat to 320°F (160°C) and bake for 30 minutes more, or until an inserted toothpick comes out clean. Remove from cake pan and cool to room temperature.

7. For garnish, from one carrot, cut 6–8 pieces (like miniature carrots) about 1–inch (2½–cm) long and cook in boiling water until tender. Sprinkle the top center of the cake with the confectioners' sugar. Using the bits of the parsley to look like carrot leaves, decorate cake top with miniature carrots.

# *Japanese Pizza by the Fire*

*What better way to relax with friends after an active day than to eat and drink, with frequent visits to the cooking table laid out with vegetables and delicately sliced meat or seafood? Fun to assemble and quick to cook according to your guests' preferences, without much ado the chef can make skillet pizzas to order.*

**Japanese Pizza**
**Green Salad with Lemon–Soy Dressing**
**Orange Basket Gelatin**

## **Japanese Pizza** *(Okonomi–yaki)*

*There are imaginative combinations of toppings and sauces possible for Japanese pizza. Your creativity can even be inspired by leftovers in the refrigerator incorporated into surprising palate–pleasers. The ingredients can either be pre–stirred into the basic pizza batter or can be added on top of the cooking pizza crust. Mayonnaise and ketchup are popular standby sauces—and for good reason: they go marvelously well with any of the pizzas. Here they are enhanced with other savory ingredients.*

*1) Shrimp, red and yellow peppers and daikon sprouts (kaiware). Serve with curry–mayonnaise sauce.*

*2) Short–necked clams, bean sprouts, bonito flakes (katsuo bushi) and parsley. Serve with ketchup–mustard sauce or onion–soy sauce.*

*3) Apple, pineapple and prunes. Serve with mayonnaise or onion–soy sauce.*

*4) Beef, cabbage, brown mushrooms, spring onion and ginger. Serve with ketchup–worcestershire sauce.*

*5) Shrimp, white mushrooms and mixed vegetables. Serve with onion–soy sauce or curry–mayonnaise sauce.*

*6) Chicken, green and red peppers, and bean sprouts. Serve with ketchup–mustard sauce or onion–soy sauce.*

*7) Pork, apple, cabbage and raisins. Serve with onion–soy sauce or curry–mayonnaise sauce.*

*8) Pork, cabbage, sesame seeds, shiso and ginger. Serve with ketchup–mustard sauce or onion–soy sauce.*

### *Ingredients (6 servings or eighteen 5–inch [12½–cm] pizzas)*

**Crust:**

4 cups (480 g) all–purpose flour
1½ tsps baking powder
1/2 tsp salt
2 beaten eggs
2 cups water
vegetable oil for greasing skillet

**Toppings (quantities indicated for each kind of topping make 6 very small pizzas):**

a) Beef, ginger, cabbage and daikon sprouts (kaiware):
3½ oz (100 g) beef; loin, fillet or round, ground or sliced into thin, 1/3–inch (1–cm) square pieces
half–a–thumb size ginger root, chopped fine
1 cabbage leaf, cut into fine strips
1/3 package (1 oz / 28 g) daikon sprouts (if unavailable, use an equivalent amount of watercress leaves)

Serve with ketchup–worcestershire sauce

b) Pork, cabbage and sesame seeds:
3½ oz (100 g) pork; loin or leg, ground or sliced into thin, 1/3–inch (1–cm) squares
1 cabbage leaf, cut into fine strips
2 or 3 shiso leaves, chopped fine
half–a–thumb size ginger root, chopped fine
2 tsps sesame seeds for garnish

Serve with ketchup–worcestershire sauce or onion–soy sauce

c) Chicken, eggs and green onion:
3½ oz (100 g) chicken, sliced into thin, 1/3–inch (1–cm) squares
1 green onion, sliced thin diagonally
6 eggs, broken directly onto each pizza crust

Serve with curry–mayonnaise sauce or ketchup–worcestershire sauce

**Sauces:**

**Ketchup–Worcestershire sauce:**

1/2 cup ketchup
1/4–1/5 cup Japanese Worcestershire sauce
1–2 tsps mustard

**Curry–Mayonnaise sauce:**

1 cup mayonnaise
1 Tbsp curry powder
2 tsps grated onion
2 tsps lemon juice
1 tsp soy sauce

**Onion–Soy sauce:**

1/3 cup soy sauce
2 Tbsps honey
2 Tbsps grated onion
1 Tbsp sake or dry white wine
a few dashes pepper

### *Method*

1. For crust, sift the flour, baking powder and salt together. Mix the beaten eggs with the measured water, and gradually add to flour, using a whisk to make a smooth paste. Cover with plastic wrap and let sit for 30 minutes in the refrigerator. This is the basic batter.

2. Pour 1 ladle–full of batter onto preheated and lightly greased skillet over medium–high heat. Sprinkle topping of your choice over pizza while crust is still setting. When the underside of the crust has become light brown and edges are dry, carefully turn over and cook until the topping on the other side is well done, for 2–3 minutes. With the spatula, press the crust to the skillet now and then to help cook quickly and evenly. Flip the batter–side down again, and baste the face–up topping side with suggested accompanying sauce before eating. For pizza with egg, make an indentation in the topping mixture and break an egg into it. When the egg is slightly cooked, gently flip the topping side face down onto the skillet, to cook until done to the diner's preference. Alternatively, you might break the egg directly onto the skillet next to the cooking crust, let it cook to a firm "sunny–side up," place it face down on the topping side of the pizza and then baste with sauce.

Or, for novel taste sensations, you can mix topping ingredients right into the batter: In a bowl, mix 1 ladle of batter with ingredients for selected topping, then cook in skillet as described at the beginning of this step.

*1) Pour a ladle full of batter onto preheated, lightly greased skillet.*

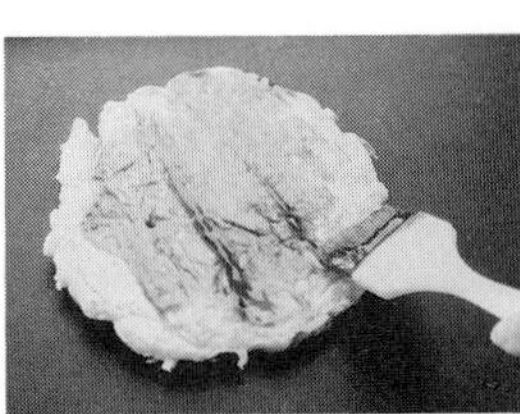

*2) Baste with a sauce.*

# Green Salad with Lemon–Soy Dressing

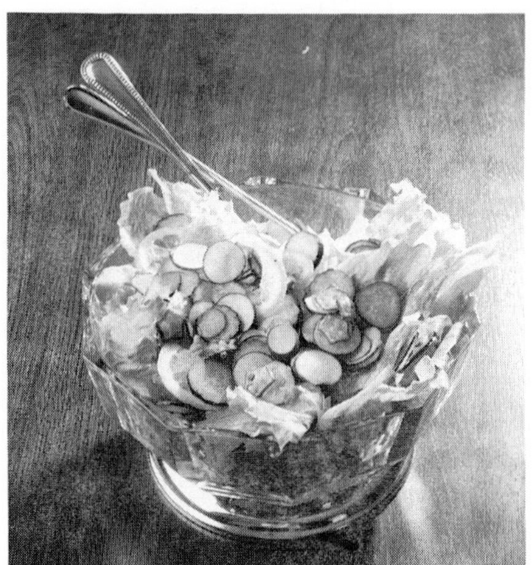

*A pungent and refreshing accompaniment permeated with lemony zest, guaranteed to wake up the taste buds.*

***Ingredients (6 servings)***

| |
|---|
| 1 head lettuce, torn into bite–size pieces |
| 1 or 2 cucumbers, sliced thin |
| 1 package okra, boiled in salted water for 1 minute, drained and sliced thin |
| 5–6 radishes, stems discarded, sliced thin |
| 1 lemon, sliced thin |

**Dressing:**

| |
|---|
| 2/3 cup vegetable oil |
| 1/2 cup rice vinegar or slightly diluted cider vinegar |
| 1/2 tsp salt |
| 1 tsp soy sauce |
| 1 Tbsp lemon juice, freshly squeezed |
| pepper to taste |

*Method*

1. Prepare vegetables.

2. Except for the oil, mix dressing ingredients and wait until the salt dissolves. Add oil gradually, mixing vigorously with a whisk until dressing is smooth. Just before serving, toss vegetables with dressing, and garnish with lemon slices.

# Orange Basket Gelatin

*Sweet juicy oranges are transformed into a light dessert, pleasingly cool and smooth.*

***Ingredients (6 servings)***

| |
|---|
| 6 oranges to make 1½–1⅔ cups (350–400 ml) orange juice |
| 1 cup water or less (to bring about 2½ cups [600 ml] of liquid with the orange juice) |
| 2 Tbsps (1/2 oz / 15 g) gelatin powder |
| 1/2 cup (120 ml) water (to moisten gelatin powder) |
| 1/2 cup (125 g) sugar |
| 2 Tbsps orange Curaçao (or other orange–flavored liqueur) |
| mint leaves as garnish |

*Method*

1. Cut 1/4 of the crown of each orange to make "cups," and squeeze out juice without tearing the peel. Using a spoon, scrape away orange segments from inside cups, being careful not to break the peel. Set aside cups and juice.

2. Add up to one cup of water to the orange juice for a total of 2½ measuring cups of liquid (600 ml). In a pan, heat to lukewarm a ladle–full of the liquid combined with sugar until the latter dissolves. Pour in the remaining orange juice–water mixture and the Curaçao.

3. In a metal bowl, add the gelatin powder gradually to measured water, and let stand until powder is completely moistened. Heat over low flame in a double boiler until gelatinous, then remove from heat and add to the mixture in step 2, stirring constantly. Pour into the orange–peel cups, almost to the brims, then chill in the refrigerator until set (for about 2 hours). Garnish with mint leaves before serving.

# An East–West Soirée

*With contrasts between aesthetic display and dramatic flavors, East and West mingle on your favorite set of dishes. Quick and easily prepared Japanese roast beef, the main dish, contend with flower–like fried fish morsels for the center of attention at this buffet table.*

**Spinach Nori Rolls**
**Tofu Purée Soup**
**Fried Fish Chrysanthemum**
**Grilled Rare Beef**
**Crab and Cucumber Salad in Lemon Cups**
**Pumpkin and Tofu Mousse**
**Dinner Rolls or Steamed Rice**

## Spinach Nori Rolls

*A healthy, low–calorie appetizer—red beets and white cottage cheese pose a gorgeous contrast with spinach morsels wrapped in black nori with orange carrot fillings.*

### *Ingredients (2 rolls)*

10 oz (280 g) spinach

1/2 carrot (one whole long carrot, cut in half lengthwise)

2 sheets nori (dried seaweed)

soy sauce, as condiment if desired

**Trimmings:**

6 oz (170 g) cottage cheese

1 can beets (sliced thin)

**Vinegar mixture for beets:**

2 tsps sugar

2 Tbsps rice vinegar or slightly diluted cider vinegar

*Method*

1. Submerge spinach stems in lightly salted boiling water, uncovered, and cook 1 minute before pushing in the leafy tops. Then cook 1 more minute, drain in a colander, and cool quickly under cold running water. Gently squeeze out excess water, then cut off stem tips. Wrap in a few layers of paper towel to remove remaining moisture. Unwrap and divide into 2 equal bunches, alternating leafy tops and stem ends to pile up an even thickness.

2. Lengthwise, cut the carrot in 6–8 fine strips, and cook in boiling water for 1 minute, drain and pat dry. (Use 3 or 4 carrot strips per spinach nori roll. One carrot will suffice for 2 rolls.)

3. To roll, place the nori with the shiny, smooth side facing down on an aluminum foil sheet (or preferably, if available, on a bamboo mat used for rolling sushi). After having enfolded 3 or 4 carrot strips within each of the two spinach bunches, position one bunch roughly 1 inch (2½ cm) from the nori edge, and then roll to the other end compressing with the foil or mat. Unwrap.

It is best to roll just before serving, or the nori may become too soggy and tear. Roll the second spinach bunch, and cut each roll into 1/2–inch (1½–cm) thick rounds. Eat with a few drops of soy sauce.

4. Soak sliced beets in the vinegar mixture seasoning for 15–20 minutes, then drain. In a platter's center, garnish the beet slices with cottage cheese, and encircle the beets with the spinach nori rounds, around the perimeter.

## Tofu Purée Soup *(Tofu no surinagashi–jiru)*

*Diced tofu in miso soup, a classic of tofu cookery, becomes transformed by purêed tofu. Thicker than consommé but lighter than cream or potage soup, ginger's subtle aroma wafts hints of the East across your dining table.*

### *Ingredients (6 servings)*

2 blocks silken tofu

1½ tsps cornstarch, dissolved in 1 Tbsp water

1 or 2 green onions (green parts only), chopped fine

2 Tbsps cornflakes as garnish

1 Tbsp ginger juice (grate ginger root and squeeze out juice with your fingers)

**Broth:**

5 cups (1200 ml) dashi (bonito stock, see page 36 "How to make dash")

5½ Tbsps light or dark brown miso (modify quantity according to the miso's saltiness)

*Method*

1. Break the tofu coarsely and purée in a mixer or blender. Add the dissolved cornstarch, then blend well again.

2. Heat the dashi to a boil and add tofu purée, stirring continuously until the broth has thickened. Cook 1 minute more, then add miso (see page 36). Sprinkle with green onions. Serve hot in individual bowls topped with 1/2 teaspoon ginger juice and 1 teaspoon cornflakes per serving.

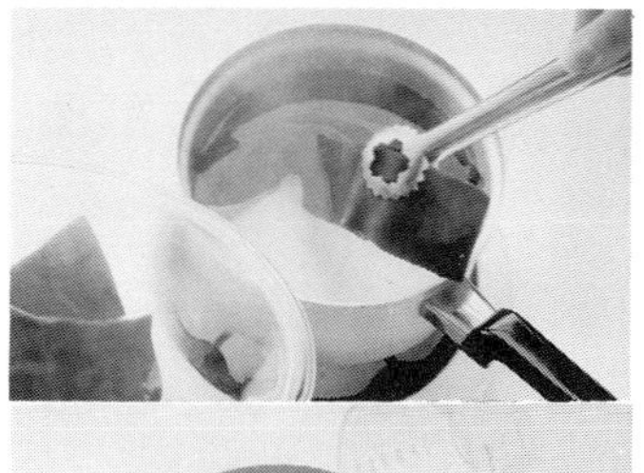

1. Remove kelp from broth.

2. Add water to stop the boiling.

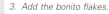

3. Add the bonito flakes.

4. Strain the broth.

5. Add the tofu purée to broth.

# Fried Fish Chrysanthemum *(Kikka–age)* 

*Like delicate ethereal ribbons, these Chinese cellophane "vermicelli" noodles enwrap fish (or chicken, if you prefer) with bright gastronomic mystery. Your guests will certainly ask, "How pretty! What is it made of?"*

### *Ingredients (6 servings)*

10 oz (280 g) swordfish, bones and skin removed

1 Tbsp sake mixed with 1/4 tsp salt, for seasoning

1 egg, (scrambled with a pinch of salt) as garnish

chrysanthemum leaves (if unavailable, use uncooked spinach leaves), as garnish

3–4 cups vegetable oil for deep–frying

**Coating:**

flour for dusting fish

1 egg, mixed with 1 Tbsp water

3½ oz (100 g) Chinese dried vermicelli (cellophane noodles), cut with scissors into 1/3–inch (1–cm) lengths

**Dipping sauce:**

2/3 cup soy sauce

1/3 cup rice vinegar or slightly diluted cider vinegar

1 Tbsp grated ginger root, added just before eating

### *Method*

1. Cut the swordfish into 1/2–inch (1½cm) square pieces, and season with salt and sake for 10 minutes. Drain and pat dry.

2. Lightly dust fish with flour, then dip in mixture of egg and water. Next, cover with Chinese vermicelli, pressing it into the coating, then wait 4–5 minutes to let the coating layers stick well.

3. Heat vegetable oil in a heavy skillet to 340°F (170°C), and gently add some of the fish. Fry only 6–7 pieces at a time. The moment the vermicelli covering comes into contact with the hot oil, it will spread out like firecracker sparkles, forming the shape of a chrysanthemum flower. When the coating has become a crispy ivory color, turn the fish over and cook about half a minute more. Avoid overcooking which would make the pieces brown and excessively oily. Drain on paper toweling or on a wire rack. Fry remaining fish pieces in the same way. Spoon 1/2 teaspoon scrambled egg on each fried piece to look like stamen, and serve hot. Border the platter's edge with chrysanthemum leaves.

4. Combine dipping sauce ingredients and, just before serving, mix in grated ginger. Have guests dip fried fish pieces in sauce before eating.

*1) Cut cellophane noodles (Chinese vermicelli) with scissors.*

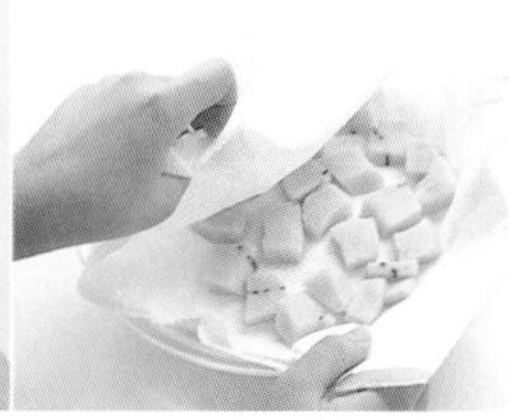

*2) After seasoning, pat fish dry with paper towels.*

*3) Press fish with Chinese vermicelli.*

*4) Take fried pieces out using tongs.*

## Grilled Rare Beef *(Gyuniku no tataki)*

*Japanese–style roast beef is sublime and fast—only 15 minutes to cook, instead of 50!*

***Ingredients (6 servings)***

2¼ lbs (1 kg) beef, loin or round, in block roughly 3 inches (7½ cm) in diameter

salt and pepper, to season beef

2–3 Tbsps vegetable oil

1 Tbsp sake and 2 Tbsps soy sauce, mixed, to season beef while sautéing

extra vegetable oil (for greasing frying pan lightly)

**Dipping sauce:**

1/2 cup soy sauce

2 tsps rice vinegar or slightly diluted cider vinegar

2 tsps mirin

**Condiments:**

half–a–thumb size ginger root, grated

2 cloves garlic, grated

2 or 3 green onions, chopped fine

10 Japanese green shiso leaves, chopped fine (if unavailable, use the leafy sections of 3 or 4 stalks of watercress)

2/3 cup grated daikon (white radish)

*Method*

1. Using your fingers, sprinkle and rub salt and pepper onto the beef, then let it stand for 20 minutes.

2. Brush sides of beef with measured oil. Heat a greased frying pan, and sauté beef until light brown all over. Brush with the mixture of sake and soy sauce, and continue sautéing.until all the sides have been browned and seasoned, for a total of 10–12 minutes. On a wire rack, cool and let excess gravy drip. Slice thin. Combine dipping sauce ingredients. Have guests dip slices of beef in sauce with selected condiments before eating.

## Crab and Cucumber Salad in Lemon Cups 

*Wakame, a high–nutrition, low–caloric sea vegetable enriches this enticing seafood salad. For everyday meals, serve in a large salad bowl.*

***Ingredients (6 servings)***

6 lemons

6 oz (170 g) crab meat, canned or boiled with shells discarded (or 5 sticks imitation crab meat)

1 cucumber, sliced thin crosswise

1 celery stalk, strings removed, sliced diagonally into bite-size pieces

1/3 oz (10 g) fresh or 1/10 oz (3 g) dried and pre-cut wakame seaweed

3 cups water, for soaking wakame

1 Tbsp lemon juice, to season crab meat (squeezed from lemons above)

**Dressing:**

3 Tbsps mayonnaise

1/2 tsp soy sauce

2 Tbsps lemon juice (squeezed from lemons above)

a pinch of salt

*Method*

1. Cut each lemon to form a basket shape, and scoop out segments, squeezing out juice to measure at least 3 tablespoons in all.

2. Remove any cartilage from crab, break coarsely, then season with the lemon juice.

3. Soak the celery slices in cold water for 4 or 5 minutes, then drain. Set aside celery leaves for garnishing.

4. Soak fresh or dried wakame in measured water until expanded, for 10–15 minutes, and then cut into pieces ranging between a half inch and one inch square (1½ to 2½ cm). (Dried and pre–cut wakame usually comes in this size.) In a colander, pour boiling hot water over wakame to clean and fix the fresh green color.

5. Mix dressing ingredients together. Just before serving, mound in lemon baskets. Arrange celery leaves on the serving platter, around the baskets.

## Pumpkin and Tofu Mousse

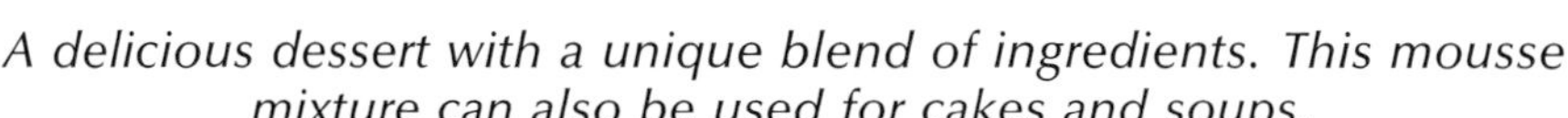

*A delicious dessert with a unique blend of ingredients. This mousse mixture can also be used for cakes and soups.*

***Ingredients (6 1–cup–size puddings)***

1 lb (450 g) acorn squash or pumpkin

2 Tbsps (15 g) gelatin powder

1/2 cup (120 ml) water to moisten gelatin powder

1 block silken tofu, roughly 10½ oz (300 g)

5 Tbsps plain, unsweetened yogurt

1/4 cup (4 Tbsps) fresh cream

2½ Tbsps honey or 1/3 cup (80 g) sugar

1 Tbsp brandy

1 Tbsp lemon juice

a few dashes of vanilla extract and nutmeg powder to taste

vegetable oil, for greasing pudding cups

**Garnish:**

1/4 cup (4 Tbsps) fresh cream

2 Tbsps sugar

6 fresh cherries (or 3 candied cherries, cut in halves)

mint leaves

*Method*

1. Scoop out and discard the seeds from the acorn squash or pumpkin, and cut into 1½–inch (4–cm) square pieces. Steam in a steamer over high heat until tender, for 10–12 minutes, then peel and discard the skin. Mash while hot.

2. Moisten the gelatin powder in measured water, then melt in a double boiler.

3. Break tofu coarsely and purée in a mixer or a blender together with mashed squash, honey (or sugar) and yogurt. Stir in vanilla extract, nutmeg, lemon juice and brandy, then gradually blend in melted gelatin.

4. Whip fresh cream until soft peaks form and fold into the mixture. Pour this mixture into each pre–greased pudding cup (or suitable serving glass). Refrigerate until set, for 3 hours, then unmold.

5. For garnishing, in another bowl, whip the fresh cream until soft peaks form. Fold in sugar, gradually, beating vigorously until peaks are stiff. Just before serving, pipe out the whipped cream in the center of each pudding, and garnish with cherries and mint leaves. Serve cold.

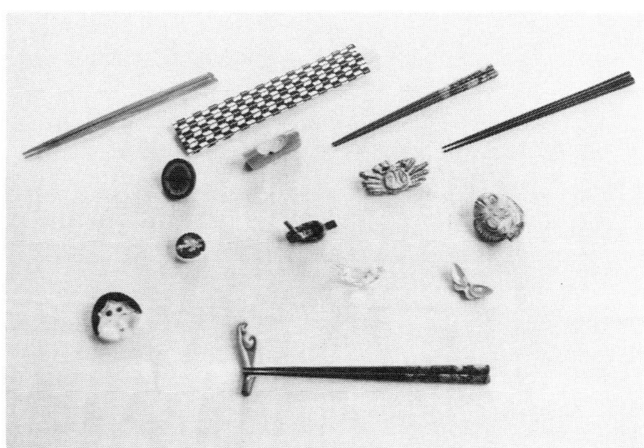

## Place Settings with Chopsticks

While Japanese-style chopsticks (or *hashi*) come in a wide variety of materials, they are all customarily narrow, with pointed ends. Although lacquer chopsticks are beautiful, they are a bit tricky since food held at the end tends to slip more easily. For beginners, wooden ones may be best.

In Japan, chopsticks are placed on chopstick rests or wrapped in a sheath at each place setting. Custom dictates that they are never allowed to come in direct contact with the table or place mat. Chopstick rests, small ornamental objects on which to place chopsticks between courses, come in many interesting designs, often shaped like flowers, animals, birds, or traditional Japanese craft patterns. Materials used include porcelain, glass and pottery as well as plain or lacquered wood. If nothing else is available, you might even use flower stems or delicate twigs! If wrapping chopsticks, fold decorative paper, such as Japanese washi, lengthwise in thirds, then fold one end before inserting chopsticks (see Tempura, p. 89).

# A Romantic Dinner for Two

*A wonderful, speedy pasta dish popular in Japan that has not yet found its way onto Western dinner tables. Pretty, snacky vegetable accompaniments are easily prepared ahead of time, letting you linger though a leisurely evening—culminating in a luscious, very special cheese cake.*

**Stuffed Belgian Endives**
**Tarako Spaghetti**
**Tomato and Daikon Canapés**
**Tofu Cheese Cake**

## Stuffed Belgian Endives

*The intriguingly bitter taste of endive complements two flavorful fillings: Oriental ground meat and scrambled ham and eggs.*

### *Ingredients (2 servings)*

8 separated endive leaves

1 head broccoli, cooked for about 5 minutes in lightly salted boiling water, drained and separated into bite–size florets

**Fillings:**

**a) Oriental meat:**

3½ oz (100 g) lean ground pork or beef

2 dried shiitake mushrooms

1/3 cup soaking water from dried mushrooms with a pinch of sugar

2 oz (60 g) canned bamboo shoots, chopped fine

1 Tbsp chopped green onions

1/2 tsp chopped ginger

1/2 tsp cornstarch, dissolved in 1 tsp water

2 tsps chopped chives, for garnish

vegetable oil for greasing frying pan

**Seasoning:**

1/2 tsp sugar

1 tsp sake

1 tsp soy sauce

1 tsp miso

**b) Scrambled ham and eggs:**

2 eggs, scrambled with a pinch of salt

2 Tbsps chopped ham

1 Tbsp mayonnaise

2 tsps cooked, chopped carrot, as garnish

*Method:*

1. For the Oriental meat filling, prepare shiitake mushrooms. Soak until spongy in 1/2 cup lukewarm water with the sugar (about 10–15 minutes). Squeeze out excess water, discard stems, and then chop fine. Reserve 1/3 cup of the soaking water to use for cooking meat.

2. Heat a lightly greased frying pan, and sauté ginger and green onions for half a minute; then add ground meat, mushrooms and bamboo shoots. Stir fry until meat becomes light in color, continuously breaking up lumps. Then add soaking water from the mushrooms along with the seasoning, and stir well. Add dissolved cornstarch and stir to thicken the gravy, cooking 1 minute.

3. For the egg filling, prepare very moist scrambled eggs and mix with mayonnaise and chopped ham.

4. To assemble, mound 2 tablespoons of the meat filling into the hollow of each of 4 Belgian endive leaves and top with chives. Into each of the other 4 leaves, spoon the egg filling, and garnish with chopped carrot. Arrange stuffed leaves like wheel–spokes radiating from the broccoli florets in the center of the platter.

## Tarako Spaghetti 

*For the pasta lover: a unique palette of colors and flavors from Japan. Sake and lemon are included for a milder taste. Besides shiso and nori, try parmesan cheese or some other favorite topping ingredient as an accent.*

***Ingredients (2 servings)***

10 oz (280 g) spaghetti, uncooked

2 tsps salt, for boiling pasta

1 tsp vegetable oil

3 pieces (6 Tbsps) tarako (salted cod roe sac)

1½ Tbsps sake

2 tsps lemon juice

6 green shiso leaves (if unavailable, use 2 Tbsps chopped green onion [green parts only]), for garnish

1/2 sheet nori, cut in 2–inch (5–cm) long fine strips with scissors, for garnish

*Method*

1. Cut tips off tarako pieces and cut in halves crosswise. Using the back of the cutting knife, squeeze out the tiny eggs inside. Add sake and lemon juice to the roe and mix well.

2. Cut shiso leaves in half lengthwise, then cut in fine strips crosswise.

3. In plenty of salted boiling water, cook spaghetti until *al dente*, 9–11 minutes (follow directions on the package).
Drain and immediately coat with oil (or oil can be added to the cooking water at the last minute). While spaghetti is still hot, mix with tarako paste. Sprinkle with strips of shiso leaves and nori: serve immediately.

## Tomato and Daikon Canapés

*Using ready–made ingredients, these 4 toppings can be made in no time. Devise and arrange your own inspired toppings—and play with the designs on each "vegetable board."*

***Ingredients (2 servings)***

1–2 tomatoes, sliced in 1/3–inch (8–mm) thick rounds

2 slices daikon (white radish), roughly 1/6–inch (4–mm) thick rounds

**Toppings**

**For tomato canapés:**

a) 4 Tbsps cottage cheese
   2 tsps chopped walnuts

b) 4 Tbsps mashed potatoes (since only a small quantity is needed, ready-prepared potato-flakes can be used, adding hot water or milk as indicated on package)

1 Tbsp frozen mixed vegetables (corn, green peas and carrot), cooked for 1 minute in lightly salted boiling water

c) 1/2 onion, sliced into thin rings
2 Tbsps dried bonito flakes *(katsuo-bushi)*
2 tsps toasted sesame seeds

**Rice–Vinaigrette dressing:**
1 Tbsp rice vinegar
2 Tbsps vegetable oil
pinch of sugar
pinch of salt
1/4 tsp mustard
pepper to taste

**For daikon canapés:**
4 Tbsps canned tuna, flaked
a few drops soy sauce
1 tsp chopped fresh chives

*Method*
1. Place each separate topping (a), b) and c)) attractively onto tomato slices. Spoon dressing over onion–ring topping before eating.

2. Soften daikon slices by soaking in lightly salted water, for 5–6 minutes, then drain and pat dry. Top with tuna and chopped fresh chives.

*Use the back side of a knife to squeeze the roe out of the skin.*

# Tofu Cheese Cake

*Not even true cheese cake connoisseurs can tell that this cake has only half the customary amount of cream cheese.*

***Ingredients (one cake 7–inch [18–cm])***
**Crust:**
2/3 cup (100 g) finely crushed graham crackers
1¾ oz (50 g) butter or margarine

**Filling:**
1 block firm tofu, excess moisture removed (see page 24)
5¼ oz (150 g) cream cheese
2 eggs, separated
2 Tbsps honey or 3 Tbsps sugar
grated rind from 1/2 lemon
1 Tbsp lemon juice
3–4 drops vanilla extract

**For optional garnish:**
2 slices tofu, 1/3 inch (1 cm) in thickness, excess moisture removed

*Method*
1. Preheat oven to 340°F (170°C). For crust, combine and knead together crushed graham crackers and butter or margarine using your fingers, and press firmly to line the inside of a round cake pan. Refrigerate until set, 20–30 minutes.

2. Bring cream cheese to room temperature. When softened, cream with a wooden spoon or spatula. Separate egg yolks from whites. Purée filling ingredients with egg yolks with a whisk or in a mixer or blender. Whip egg whites until stiff and fold into the pureéd mixture. Pour over crust and smooth the surface with a rubber spatula. Bake for about 25 minutes (test for doneness with a toothpick).

3. For optional garnish, dice tofu (1/4–inch / 8–mm pieces) and decorate the edges after the cake has cooled.

# An Elegant Luncheon

*Centering mainly on seafoods, this menu also presents twelve different kinds of vegetables, including an array of mushrooms, for a healthy, light and very elegant lunch.*

**Egg Custard with Chicken and Vegetables**
**Mushroom and Beef Salad**
**Salmon Rice**
**Pickled Turnips Chrysanthemum**
**Tofu Mellow Pudding**

# Egg Custard with Chicken and Vegetables
## (Chawan–mushi) 

*Unlike sweetened dessert puddings, this classic Japanese custard is served as a savory entrée. The subtle steamed egg broth usually contains many colorful ingredients, and this recipe includes seven: chicken, shrimp, fish cake, ginkgo nuts, mushrooms, carrot and spinach. A delicate, smooth texture results from just a little bit of care in the steaming process.*

### Ingredients (6 servings)

9 beaten eggs

6 cups (900 ml) dashi (see page 36)

1 Tbsp mirin

2½ tsps salt

1 Tbsp soy sauce

7 oz (200 g) boneless chicken breast or fillet, all skin and fat removed

6 shrimp, deveined and heads removed

1 stick chikuwa (tubular fish cake), cut into thin rings (if unavailable, use 1/2 stick kamaboko fish cake or crab meat)

6 thin slices carrot, cut into flower shapes using a cookie cutter

6 fresh (or reconstituted dried) shiitake mushrooms, stems removed, whole or cut in halves

12 ginkgo nuts (optional), canned or vacuum packed

3–4 stalks spinach

several fine strips lemon rind per serving as garnish

**Seasoning for chicken:**

2 tsps sake

a generous pinch of salt

*Method*

1. Heat dashi, mirin, salt and soy sauce until the salt has dissolved. Cool to room temperature, then mix well with beaten eggs. Strain the mixture through a fine sieve or cheesecloth to eliminate lumpiness and to achieve a smooth consistency.

2. Using a cutting knife at an angle, cut the chicken into 1/2–inch (1½–cm) pieces. Add seasoning and let stand for 10 minutes. (Using the knife at an angle results in tenderer slices.)

3. Peel the shrimp, but leave the tail and the last section of the shell nearest it intact.

4. With stem sections immersed, cook the spinach in lightly salted boiling water for 1 minute, then submerge leafy sections for an additional minute. Drain and rinse under cold running water. Squeeze out excess water, discard stems, then cut in 1–inch (2½–cm) lengths. Divide into 6 equal portions.

5. Lightly moisten the bottom of each serving cup or bowl with the egg mixture to prevent other ingredients from sticking to the container when steamed. Place the ingredients (except lemon rind) into each bowl attractively, shrimp near the top. Gently pour egg mixture into each container to about 1/3 inch (under 1 cm) below the edge of the containers.

6. Fill a steamer with water and heat to a boil over high heat. Remove from heat and insert custard cups or bowls, leaving space between them to allow steam to circulate. Cook 1 minute over high heat, covered, then reduce to very low heat. (Too high a temperature will make the surface of the custard rough or spongy, and less tasty. While steaming, insert a dry dish towel under the cover so that condensed steam will not drip onto the egg custard surface.) Loosen the steamer cover to keep at a low simmer (just below boiling point). After reducing heat, continue steaming for about 20 minutes. The custard is done when a fine skewer inserted into the

middle comes up clean. Serve hot with strips of lemon rind on top.

**Note:** If you're using an oven instead of a steamer, fill the oven pan 1/2 inch (1½ cm) deep with hot water. Place the custard cups or bowls covered with aluminum foil into the water–covered oven pan, and bake at 320°F (160°C) for 20–25 minutes.

*Strain the dashi and egg mixture through a fine sieve or cheesecloth.*

## Mushroom and Beef Salad

*One of the simplest and most quickly prepared mushroom dishes. Here beef provides a major accent, but this recipe is also delicious when made only with mushrooms. A sprinkling of corn kernels on top gives a nice splash of color.*

### *Ingredients (6 servings)*

- 2 pkgs (7 oz / 200 g) shimeji mushrooms, bottoms trimmed and separated into bite–size clusters
- 6 fresh (or reconstituted dried) shiitake mushrooms, tops only, cut into fine strips
- 10 Western white mushrooms, tops only, sliced thin, then sprinkled with lemon juice
- 2 pkgs (7 oz / 200g) enokidake mushrooms, with 1 inch (2½ cm) of stems cut off
- 3½ oz (100 g) beef, loin or round, sliced thin and cut into bite–size pieces
- 1 head chicory, escarole or romaine lettuce, rinsed and torn into bite–size pieces
- 1/4 cup water
- 1 Tbsp vegetable oil for sautéing

**Seasoning:**

- 3 tsps sake
- 3 tsps soy sauce
- a generous pinch of salt

**Garnish:**

- 2 Tbsps frozen corn
- 2 Tbsps frozen green peas (cook corn and peas according to package instructions together in lightly salted boiling water)

### *Method*

Sauté the beef in a preheated frying pan with 1 teaspoon oil for 1 minute (until the color is a pale gray), then season with 1 teaspoon each sake and soy sauce. Remove beef from the pan and set aside. Add 2 teaspoons oil to the pan, and sauté shimeji mushrooms for 1 minute. Add measured water, then add shiitake and white mushrooms, stirring continuously. Season with salt, 2 teaspoons each sake and soy sauce. Finally add enokidake mushrooms and cooked beef, and mix well. Remove from heat. Enokidake mushrooms will stay crisp if you avoid over–cooking. Serve warm, surrounded by lettuce, and garnish with corn and green peas.

## Salmon Rice *(Sake gohan)*

*The taste, aroma and color of this beautiful, easy–to–prepare rice dish make it perfect for entertaining. Rich, succulent salmon embellished with sesame, ginger and green shiso will inspire admiration at the table.*

### *Ingredients (6 servings)*

- 3 cups (600 g) short grain rice
- 3⅓ cups (800 ml) water

**Seasoning:**

2/3 tsp salt

2 Tbsps sake

3 fillets salmon, roughly 10 oz (280 g) in all

3½ oz (100 g) fresh green beans

pinch of salt (for cooking green beans)

10 green shiso leaves, cut into fine strips

3 Tbsps toasted sesame seeds

1 thumb–size piece ginger root, peeled, chopped fine, soaked in water and drained

*Method*

1. Cook the rice with seasoning (see page 14 "How to cook rice")

2. Grill the salmon over a low flame until cooked (about 3–4 minutes per side). Remove any skin and bones (after grilling), then break into large flakes with fingers.

3. Trim green beans, and cook in lightly salted boiling water for about 2 minutes, or until tender. Drain and cool quickly under cold running water, then diagonally cut each pod into thin slices.

4. Coarsely chop or grind sesame seeds. Chopping with a heavy knife over a dry dish towel will keep the seeds from scattering and will bring out their good aroma while avoiding the danger of grinding them too fine.

5. With a wet spatula, mix all ingredients except shiso leaves with hot rice, using a cutting motion. Just before serving, mix in the shiso leaves.

## Pickled Turnips Chrysanthemum *(Kikka–kabu)* 

*Each region of Japan boasts its own pickle specialty. These flower–cut turnips possess a natural sweetness and crunch, enhanced by their distinctive shape and the flavorful pickling mixture used in their preparation. These blooming chrysanthemum shapes dress up and complement the main course.*

***Ingredients (6 servings)***

6 turnips

1 dried red chili pepper, softened in water, then seeded and cut in thin rings

a generous pinch of salt, for tenderizing turnips

**Pickling mixture:**

1 Tbsp mirin

3/4 cup (180 ml) rice vinegar or slightly diluted cider vinegar

2 Tbsps sugar

1/2 tsp salt

*Method*

1. Peel turnips. Next, place a turnip between two

1/4 cup (90 g) honey

1½ cups (360 ml) milk

2 Tbsps (15 g) gelatin powder

1/2 cup water to dissolve gelatin powder

a pinch of salt

water or vegetable oil for moistening mold

**Garnish:**

1/2 cup dark cherries, fresh or canned

**Sauce:**

1/2 cup syrup from canned dark cherries (if fresh cherries, use 1/2 cup water boiled with 1/4 cup [60 g] sugar)

1 Tbsp sugar

1 tsp brandy

1 tsp cornstarch, dissolved in 2 tsps water

2. To tenderize, sprinkle turnips with salt and let sit for 10 minutes; rinse off salt and pat dry. Soak turnips in marinade for at least 1 hour (up to 2–3 hours), turning occasionally for even absorption. Before serving, drain lightly and, with fingers, spread out the "petals" to look like a chrysanthemum flower. In the center, garnish with 2 or 3 rings of chili pepper.

## Pudding 

*combines easily with sweet ingredients not accustomed to the taste of tofu, re of molasses tempered with milder ead of cherry topping, you might want r blueberry sauce.*

*Method*

1. Dissolve the gelatin powder in measured water, then melt over medium–heat in a double boiler.

2. Purée tofu, egg yolks, molasses, honey and salt together in a mixer or a blender.

3. Heat milk to lukewarm, then remove from heat and add gelatin mixture gradually, stirring continuously with a whisk. Add to the purée.

4. Beat egg whites until stiff, and by thirds, fold into the tofu mixture, taking care not to crush egg white bubbles.

5. Moisten with water (or grease with vegetable oil) the inside of a mold. Pour in mixture and chill in the refrigerator until set (this will take less than 1 hour).

6. For sauce, simmer the syrup and sugar together until sugar dissolves. Thicken by adding dissolved cornstarch, cooking half a minute. Remove from heat and stir in brandy. Chill. To serve, unmold pudding, garnish with dark cherries and pour sauce over. Any remaining sauce can be served alongside individual pudding servings.

# *Japanese Fondue*

*Make–them–yourself dishes, simmering right on the dining table, are naturally popular in cold weather. This oil "fondue," however, will gather a crowd in any season. Each guest spears and prepares his or her own delectable choices, enjoying them freshly cooked and crackling hot. An elegant gelatin dessert ends this satisfying meal with a delightful flourish.*

**Japanese Fondue**
**Spinach Salad with Potato Chip Croutons and Oriental Dressing**
**Clear Tofu Flower Soup**
**Steamed Rice**
**Coffee and Milk Jellied Delight**

# **Japanese Fondue** *(Kushi–age)*

*It's not necessary to furnish the extravagant variety of ingredients shown here; select a few from the combinations presented, or have diners spear their own combinations from among available ingredients. Cut ingredients small and thin—easy to impale with fondue forks (two pieces per fork).*

### *Ingredients (6–8 servings)*

### Suggested combinations to be threaded onto skewers:

a) Beef and asparagus (1–2 min.)
1 lb (450 g) beef (filet mignon or round) cut into bite–size chunks and seasoned lightly with salt and pepper
4 spears green asparagus, cut in 1-1/2–inch (4–cm) lengths

b) Rolled pork with apples (1 min.)
1 apple, cored and cut into thin wedges, soaked in lightly salted water for 2–3 minutes, then drained
7 oz (200 g) pork thigh or shoulder, sliced thin, then wrapped around each apple slice

c) Potatoes and bacon (1/2–1 min.)
4 medium–size potatoes, boiled and peeled, then cut into bite–size pieces
8 thin slices bacon, cut in 4–inch (10–cm) lengths, wrapped around each potato piece

d) Lotus root and ground meat (1–2 min.)
7 oz (200 g) lotus root, fresh or canned
5 oz (140 g) ground chicken, pork or beef
salt and pepper to taste
2 tsps flour
1 tsp vinegar (for soaking fresh lotus root)

If you're using fresh lotus root, peel and cut into 1/5–inch (1/2–cm) thick rounds and soak immersed in water with 1 tsp vinegar for 5 minutes. Drain and rinse off vinegar, then pat dry. Mix ground meat with salt, pepper and flour and make a paste. Press lotus root into meat mixture so that every lotus root hole is completely filled. With a spatula, smooth the sides, scraping off excess meat mixture. Spear onto a fondue fork.

Other suggested combinations: rolled pork with asparagus (1–2 minutes); chicken and fine strips of fresh ginger (1–2 min.); cooked ham and pineapple slices (several seconds); tuna and green onion (1/2 min.); shrimp and green peppers (1/2–1 min.); shiitake mushrooms and green peppers (1 min.); chicken and green onion (1–2 min.); scallops wrapped in green shiso leaves (1/2–1 min.); and acorn squash and green peppers (1 min.).

### Batter:

1 beaten egg

4/5 cup (200 ml) cold water, added to beaten egg

4/5 cup (100 g) all–purpose flour, sifted

### Coating:

About 2 cups (150 g) dry bread crumbs, ground finely in a mixer or blender, set on the table next to the batter

### Oil:

3–4 cups fresh vegetable oil for deep-frying

### Dipping sauces:

a) 1/2 cup ketchup and 1 tsp mustard, mixed

b) 1/2 cup ketchup and 1/4 cup Japanese Worcestershire sauce, mixed

c) 1/2 cup soy sauce and 1 tsp mustard, mixed

d) 1/2 cup mayonnaise and 1 Tbsp ketchup, mixed

### Seasonings:

a) salt to taste (at table)

b) 1/3 cup curry powder and 1 tsp salt, mixed

c) seven–spice pepper (shichimi)

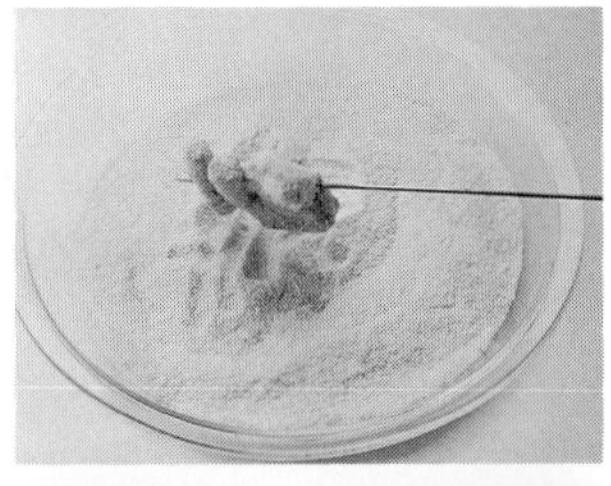

*1) Coat speared combination with ground dry bread crumbs.*

*2) Combine ingredients requiring compatible frying times.*

*Method*
Just before frying, prepare batter. Add flour to egg–water mixture, mixing with a whisk, but do not overmix. Divide into 2 separate bowls and set on the dining table within easy reach. Heat oil in a fondue pot or heavy, deep kettle to 340°F (170°C) or until it begins to smoke slightly. First, have diners immerse speared combinations in the batter, then roll in coating of ground dry bread crumbs. Deep-fry for the duration indicated (beef, a bit rare, is delicious with this short frying time). Cómbine ingredients requiring compatible frying times. (For example, you wouldn't want scallops and acorn squash on the same skewer, since the scallops would overfry by the time the acorn squash was ready.) Meat and firm vegetables can be deep–fried for 1–2 minutes; seafood and soft vegetables, 1/2–1 minute. Dip lightly in a dipping sauce or sprinkle with a seasoning before eating.

## Spinach Salad with Potato Chip Croutons and Oriental Dressing

*An easily made salad with crunch. Select spinach with beautiful fresh leaves.*

***Ingredients (6–8 servings)***

1 bundle spinach (10 oz / 280 g); use leafy sections only (stems discarded)

6–8 Western white mushrooms, stemmed and sliced thin, then sprinkled with a squeeze of lemon juice

4–5 radishes, sliced thin

1 cup potato chips, broken into bite–size, or smaller, pieces

**Oriental Dressing:**
**Whisk together the following:**

4 Tbsps rice vinegar or slightly diluted cider vinegar

4 Tbsps soy sauce

2 Tbsps mirin

1 Tbsp sesame oil

1 tsp ground sesame seeds

*Method*
Toss together all salad ingredients with dressing just before serving.

## Clear Tofu Flower Soup

*In clear soup, tofu's whiteness provides a background for setting off other more colorful ingredients. Besides carrots and green beans, you might try combining tofu with wakame seaweed and your favorite mushrooms in this fragrant broth.*

***Ingredients (6–8 servings)***

1 block silken tofu

2 oz (60 g) carrot, julienned

3 oz (85 g) green beans, trimmed

**Broth:**

6 cups dashi (see page 36)

1 tsp salt

1½ tsps soy sauce

*Method*

1. Cut the tofu into 1/3–inch (1–cm) thick slices crosswise, then cut each piece into flower shapes with a cookie cutter.

2. Cook the green beans in lightly salted boiling water for 2–3 minutes, until tender. Drain and cool under cold running water. Cut diagonally into fine strips.

3. Cook the carrot in the broth until tender (about ten minutes), then carefully add tofu flowers. When soup simmers again, turn off heat. Place green beans in each soup bowl and then gently pour in the hot soup. Serve immediately.

## Coffee and Milk Jellied Delight

*Coffee and milk transformed into a sophisticated, pretty (and not too sweet) coffee–brown, milky–white layered gelatin dessert. When serving to children, use a little less coffee and garnish with cherries instead of roasted coffee beans.*

***Ingredients: (for 6–8 individual portions)***

**Milk gelatin:**

| |
|---|
| 2 Tbsps (15 g) gelatin powder |
| 6 Tbsps (90 ml) water to dissolve gelatin powder |
| 2½ cups (600 ml) milk |
| 2/3 cup (150 g) sugar |

**Coffee gelatin:**

| |
|---|
| 2 Tbsps (15 g) gelatin powder |
| 6 Tbsps (90 ml) water to dissolve gelatin powder |
| 2½ cups (600 ml) strong coffee (regular or instant) |
| 2/3 cup (150 g) sugar |
| 4 Tbsps (60 ml) hot water to dissolve coffee powder |

**Garnish:**

| |
|---|
| 1/2 cup (120 g) fresh cream |
| 1 Tbsp (16 g) sugar |
| 6 roasted coffee beans (or, if preferred, candied cherries) |

*Method*

1. Prepare milk gelatin first. Dissolve gelatin powder in measured water. Heat milk with sugar until all the sugar has dissolved.

2. In a double boiler over medium heat, gradually add dissolved gelatin to the milk–sugar mixture. After the mixture cools, pour an equal amount of gelatin into each serving glass. Cool in the refrigerator.

3. Prepare coffee gelatin following steps 1 and 2 (using coffee instead of milk). Stir into gelatin–water mixture.

4. After refrigeration, while the surface of milk gelatin is still slightly runny (after 30 minutes), very gently pour coffee gelatin over it. (If the surface of the milk gelatin is disturbed, it will mix with and blur the coffee gelatin.) Chill in the refrigerator until set.

5. Whip fresh cream with sugar until stiff and, with a pastry tube, generously pipe out a decorative design onto the surface of each gelatin serving. Top each with a roasted coffee bean.

# *Tempura: Rising to the Challenge*

*Tempura entails coating a wide variety of ingredients with batter and then deep–frying. At first consideration, eating sashimi, or raw fish, may seem barbaric, but this dish, in fact, requires exceptionally fresh fish and impeccable preparation skills. Here, I've introduced ready–to–use ingredients, so anyone can achieve success. Miso soup, a good accompaniment to tempura, in this version contains healthy sea vegetables. Salad with a hint of hot–spiciness will be a tempting palate refreshener between bites of tempura. The subtle ice cream finale, made with the same fragrant green tea powder that is used in the Japanese tea ceremony, will linger in your guests' memories as a very special dessert.*

**Assorted Sashimi**
**Tempura**
**Miso Soup with Deep–Fried Tofu Pouches and Wakame**
**Spicy Eggplant Salad**
**Steamed Rice**
**Green Tea Ice Cream**

## Assorted Sashimi

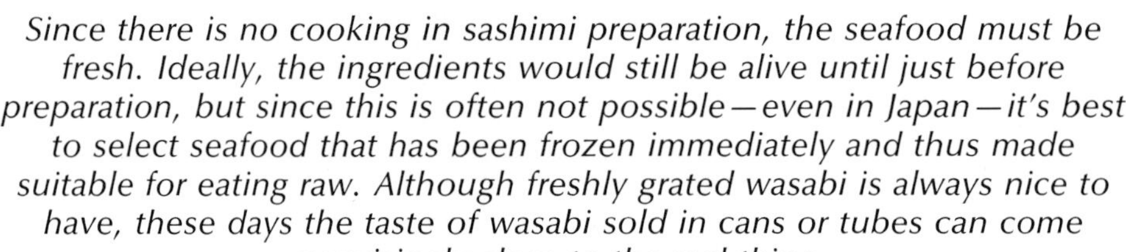
*Since there is no cooking in sashimi preparation, the seafood must be fresh. Ideally, the ingredients would still be alive until just before preparation, but since this is often not possible—even in Japan—it's best to select seafood that has been frozen immediately and thus made suitable for eating raw. Although freshly grated wasabi is always nice to have, these days the taste of wasabi sold in cans or tubes can come surprisingly close to the real thing.*

### *Ingredients (6 servings)*

10 oz (280 g) tuna sashimi fillet, fresh or frozen, cut into 2 × 1/2–inch (5 × 1½–cm) slices

7 oz (200 g) cleaned and skinned squid for sashimi, cut into slices, same as tuna

12–14 shrimp for sashimi, heads removed, shelled (but leave tail intact) and deveined

6 shucked scallops, fresh or frozen for sashimi, sliced into 2–3 rounds each

1/5 oz (5 g) dried wakame (sea vegetable) or 1 oz (28 g) fresh, salted wakame

1 or 2 kiwis, peeled and sliced thin

1 avocado, pitted and peeled, cut thin

**Complements:**

- 1/3 medium carrot (1 oz / 28 g), cut into julienne
- 3 oz (85 g) daikon (white radish), cut into julienne
- 1 large cucumber, peeled, sliced thin diagonally, then cut into julienne
- 1/2 lemon, sliced thin
- 4 inch (10 cm) green onion, cut in half crosswise, then cut lengthwise into julienne
- 3 Tbsps wasabi paste

**Dipping sauce:**

Soy sauce

*Method*

1. If you're using dried wakame, soak it in water for 10 minutes or until it expands and becomes tender. Cook in boiling water for 1 minute, then drain. Cut off any tough veins, and cut into 1-inch (2½–cm) lengths. If you're using fresh, salted wakame, rinse off salt and soak in water for 5–6 minutes before cutting.

2. Separately soak the strips of carrot, daikon and cucumber in cold water for 10 minutes to make firm, then drain.

3. Arrange all ingredients attractively on a platter. Give each guest a small saucer containing a dab of wasabi paste and soy sauce. Each person dabs a bit of wasabi paste onto sashimi, then dips, sparingly, into the soy sauce before eating. Vegetable complements can be eaten between bites of sashimi to refresh the palate.

## Tempura

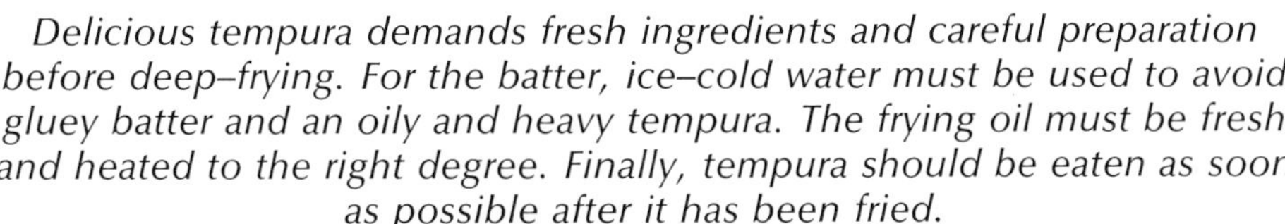

*Delicious tempura demands fresh ingredients and careful preparation before deep–frying. For the batter, ice–cold water must be used to avoid gluey batter and an oily and heavy tempura. The frying oil must be fresh and heated to the right degree. Finally, tempura should be eaten as soon as possible after it has been fried.*

***Ingredients (6 servings)***

**Seafood:**

- 6 white–meat fish (smelt or sillago), fresh or frozen, gutted and filleted to a butterfly shape
- 6 prawns, head removed, shelled (but with tail and the last section of the shell intact) and deveined
- 6 pieces squid fillets, 2 × 1–inch (5 × 2½–cm) each

**Vegetables:**

- 1 onion, cut in half lengthwise, then cut crosswise into 1/3–inch (1–cm) thick half rounds–each piece held together with a toothpick
- 7 oz (200 g) acorn squash, seeded and cut into 1/5–inch (1/2–cm) oblong pieces
- 1 medium carrot, cut into julienne
- 6 fresh (or reconstituted dried) shiitake mushrooms, stems removed
- 1 or 2 small green peppers, seeded and cut lengthwise into 6 portions each
- 1 small sweet potato, cut into 1/5–inch (1/2–cm) thick rounds (optional)
- 3½ oz (100 g) lotus root, peeled and cut into 1/5–inch (1/2–cm) thick rounds, soaked in water with 1 tsp vinegar (optional)
- 6 green shiso leaves (optional)
- 5–6 cups vegetable oil for deep frying

**Batter:**

- 1½ cup (180 g) all–purpose flour
- 4 Tbsps cornstarch
- 2 tsps baking powder
- 2 lightly beaten eggs
- 1⅗ cups ice water
- extra flour for coating

**Tentsuyu dipping sauce:**

- 2 cups dashi (bonito stock, see page 36 "How to make dashi")

6 Tbsps mirin

8 Tbsps soy sauce

**Condiments:**

10 oz (280 g) grated daikon (white radish)

1 thumb–size fresh ginger root, peeled and grated

*Method*

**To ready ingredients for deep–frying**

1. Make slits on the belly side of each prawn at three points to prevent it from curling when fried. Trim the tips of each prawn tail, and squeeze out moisture from inside each tail with the back edge of the cutting knife, to prevent spattering when fried.

2. Make several short slits on all edges of each squid fillet piece to prevent curling when fried.

3. If you're using sweet potato, soak slices in water for 5 minutes, then drain and pat dry.

4. If you're using lotus root, soak rounds in water with measured vinegar to prevent the roots from discoloring. Drain and rinse off vinegar, then pat dry.

5. Bring to a boil all the ingredients for tentsuyu dipping sauce, then remove from heat.

6. Preheat oil in a wok or a large, heavy kettle to 340°F (170°C) or until the oil begins to smoke slightly. (To tell the temperature, refer to step 8.)

7. Prepare the batter. Sift together twice the flour, cornstarch and baking powder. To beaten eggs, add measured ice water enough to make a bit more than 2 cups of liquid, and pour into a large bowl. Whisk in sifted flour mixture. The mixture may be slightly lumpy, but don't worry, the batter will eventually settle to a smooth consistency. Avoid overmixing. Keep away from any heat source which will make the batter sticky, later to result in oily, heavy–tasting fried food.

8. Test the temperature of the oil by dripping a bit of the batter into the oil. If it sinks to the bottom of the wok, the oil's temperature is not yet high enough for frying; if it sinks halfway and then floats quickly to the top, the temperature is suitable (around 340°F / 170°C) for frying vegetables. (If the batter splatters on the surface, the oil is too hot.) Begin frying vegetables first, then move on to seafoods.

**How to fry**

1. Dip acorn squash pieces, completely, in the batter, shake off excess batter and slide coated pieces into the oil. To maintain the oil temperature, avoid adding too many pieces at any one time so that they never occupy more than 2/3 of the surface of the oil. Fry until undersides have become golden brown, then turn and cook the other sides until tender, about 1 minute per side. If they brown in several seconds, the oil is too hot and additional new oil should be added to bring down the temperature. Test for doneness by sticking with a fine skewer. Remove from the oil and drain on a wire rack or on paper toweling. From the oil, skim fried batter, leftover after each fried batch. Fry onion pieces, optional lotus root and sweet potato slices in the same way. For green peppers, fry only 10 seconds per side.

2. Cover carrot strips lightly with extra flour in a bowl and coat all strips with batter (about 1/2–2/3 of a ladle). Make bunches of 6 or 7 carrot strips each, using chopsticks or a spoon, then slide into the oil, keeping separate bunches from touching and sticking to each other. After each bunch has "set" firmly, turn and fry the other

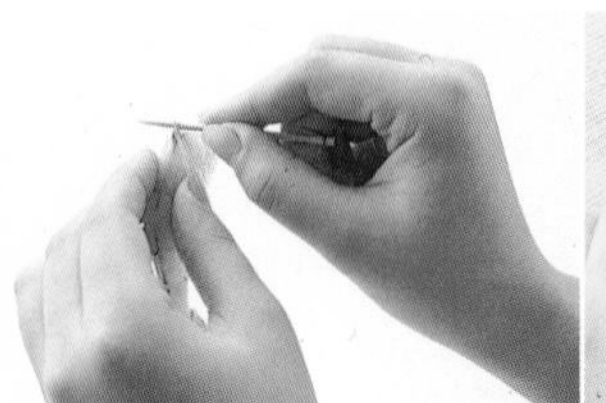

1) Devein prawns by inserting toothpick between segments.

2) Make slits at three points on the belly side of each prawn.

3) Use the back of a knife to drain water from the tail.

4) Pour the egg and water mixture into a cup to measure a bit more than 2 cups of liquid.

side for about half a minute, or until cooked to a light golden color. Drain.

3. For shiitake mushrooms, shallowly dip only the undersides of the mushroom caps into the batter. Fry the battered sides for 1 minute, then drain.

4. Holding the stem with your fingers, coat the dull side of each green shiso leaf with batter. Fry the battered sides for only a few seconds, then drain.

5. At this point, about 1/2 cup of fresh oil should be added to the wok. (Lack of oil will cause ingredients to burn before being cooked through.) Raise temperature to 360°F (180°C) for frying seafood. You can test this again by dropping a little bit of batter into the hot oil. If it sinks only slightly beneath the surface (not halfway down) and then comes up immediately, the temperature is about right. Since most seafood is moist and tender in consistency, shorter cooking time in hotter oil is necessary.

6. Lightly cover fish with extra flour. Dip in the batter, holding the tail of the fish with chopsticks or tongs. Do the same for the prawns and squid. Fry fish and squid half a minute per side and prawns 1 minute per side, then drain.

7. When all frying is completed, strain the oil through a fine sieve, lined with kitchen towel, into an oil receptacle while it is still hot. Keep in a dark, cool place. This oil can be reused 1 or 2 more times for non–tempura deep–frying, or 1 more time for sautéing.

8. Serve hot tempura on a platter or individual plates lined with paper toweling. Reheat dipping sauce and serve warm in individual dipping bowls. Serve grated daikon and ginger separately in saucers on the side for each guest to mix into the dipping sauce according to taste. Dip tempura in the sauce and eat.

## Miso Soup with Deep–Fried Tofu Pouches and Wakame

### *(Abura–age to wakame no miso–shiru)* 

*Wakame is a sea vegetable that can easily become a part of daily fare. With pre–cut wakame, preparation is easy and quick, combining harmoniously with tofu, tofu products, vegetables, chicken–practically all foods.*

***Ingredients (6 servings)***

2 deep–fried tofu pouches (*abura–age or usu–age*)

1/5 oz (5 g) dried wakame (sea vegetable) or 1 oz (28 g) fresh, salted wakame

2 Tbsps chopped green onion (green parts only) for garnish

**Broth:**

6 cups dashi (bonito stock, see page 36 "How to make dashi")

5 or 6 Tbsps miso (nonsweet)

*Method*

1. Pour boiling water on both sides of deep–fried tofu pouches to remove excess oil. Cut into halves lengthwise, then cut each piece crosswise into 1/5–inch (1/2–cm) fine strips.

2. Prepare the wakame as in step 1 for sashimi and cut into 1/2–inch (1½–cm) lengths.

3. Cook both ingredients together in dashi for 1 minute. Place miso in a strainer or small sieve, and immerse in dashi. With a spoon, stir miso until it dissolves. Bring to a boil again, add green onions, then remove from heat. Serve hot.

## Spicy Eggplant Salad 

*Chilling these eggplant slices before eating them between bites of hot tempura will make them taste even more scrumptiously pungent.*

***Ingredients (6 servings)***

4 Japanese eggplants or 2 American eggplants

salt for boiling eggplant

**Dressing:**

1 Tbsp sugar

3 Tbsps soy sauce

3 Tbsps rice vinegar or slightly diluted cider vinegar

2 tsps sesame oil

1/2 tsp Chinese hot oil (if unavailable, substitute a dried red pepper with seeds removed, chopped fine)

1 Tbsp chopped green onion or fresh chives

1 Tbsp chopped or grated ginger

**Garnishes:**

6 inch (15 cm) green onion

1 thumb–size fresh ginger root, sliced paper–thin, then cut into fine strips

1 dried red chili pepper, softened in water, then seeded and cut into thin rings

*Method*

1. Cut the eggplants in roughly 3 × 1–inch (7½ × 1½–cm) strips lengthwise, and boil in lightly salted boiling water for 1–2 minutes until tender, then drain.

2. Cut green onion into hair–thin slices lengthwise. Soak in water for 5 minutes. Drain.

3. Mix all ingredients for dressing, and put aside about 2 tablespoons for pouring over the garnishes later. 15–20 minutes before serving, lightly squeeze out excess moisture from eggplants, and mix with dressing. Pour remaining dressing over garnish: green onion, ginger root and chili pepper rings.

## Green Tea Ice Cream 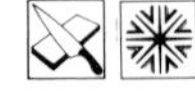

*There is nothing quite like ice cream, which goes beyond time and geographical borders as an all–around favorite dessert. The pretty green color belonging to this Japanese version reflects a refined, heavenly flavor.*

***Ingredients (about 5 cups [1200 ml] ice cream)***

2 Tbsps green tea powder

3/5 cup (150 g) sugar

1⅘ cup (450 ml) milk

1 cup (240 ml) whipping cream

4 egg yolks

1 Tbsp rum

a few drops vanilla extract

biscuits, to be served on side

*Method*

1. In a pan, heat the milk to lukewarm temperature. Mix the green tea powder with a small amount of the sugar, and stir in milk gradually until the powder has dissolved evenly. Strain through a fine sieve to remove any lumps.

2. Beat egg yolks and gradually stir in remaining sugar until creamy. Slowly stir in mixture of milk and green tea powder. Heat in a pan over low heat, stirring with a wooden spatula until creamy but still runny. When cooled to room temperature, blend in rum and vanilla extract.

3. Whisk the whipping cream until the texture is as creamy as the green tea mixture in step 2 and gradually stir in. Transfer to a metal container, and chill in the freezer. When the bottom section has frozen (after about 40–60 min.), mix entire mixture with a spoon until fluffy to let air in. Repeat this process 2 or 3 more times every 30 minutes until the ice cream has an even, creamy consistency. Serve with biscuits on the side.

*1) Mix the green tea powder with a small amount of the measured sugar.*

*2) Gradually stir in green tea powder.*

*3) Mix egg yolk mixture with the milk and green tea powder.*

# *Sukiyaki: Everybody's Favorite*

*Along with tempura and sushi, sukiyaki is another world–famous Japanese dish—eaten anytime except during the hot season. Preparing this popular one–pot meal at the table is quick and easy—mostly cutting vegetables and tofu, with no special preparation necessary for the dipping sauce. Sukiyaki's sweet–spicy taste is well balanced with the turnip salad, a refreshing accompaniment. For dessert, Western and Oriental tastes merge in a fantastic Bavarian cream.*

**Sukiyaki**
**Okra and Turnip Salad**
**Rice with Parsley**
**Green Tea Bavarian Cream**

## Sukiyaki

*In Japan, sukiyaki tastes best when made with marbled beef (where the fat is dispersed in delicate waves throughout the meat), which is the kind of meat that is used here. Lean meat works perfectly well too, of course, but it's advisable to half-freeze the block of meat first, and then slice it super–thin since it may be tougher (ask your butcher). Sukiyaki always contains shirataki (transparent "noodles" from the devil's tongue plant), but be careful to place it away from the meat in the skillet, since it tends to toughen beef. If you have guests who are reluctant to use raw eggs as a dipping sauce, dilute the cooking broth by adding a little extra water and eat the sukiyaki plain.*

***Ingredients: (for 6 servings)***

2 lbs (900 g) beef, sliced very thin (loin, tenderloin, rib roast or round)

2 blocks firm tofu or grilled tofu if available, cut into 1–inch (2½–cm) cubes, drained

6 fresh (or reconstituted dried) shiitake mushrooms, stemmed

2 packages enokidake mushrooms, with 1 inch (2½ cm) of stems cut off

1 onion, sliced into thin rings

2 green onions, sliced diagonally 1/3–inch (1–cm) thick

1 bundle (300 g) edible chrysanthemum leaves, cut into 3–4 portions (if unavailable, use 1 bunch [300 g] spinach, cut into 3–4 portions)

2 or 3 Chinese cabbage leaves (optional), cut into 1–inch (2½–cm) long pieces

1 package shirataki noodles (if unavailable, 3 oz [85 g] Chinese vermicelli can be substituted)

one 1–inch (2½–cm) cube of beef suet or 1 tsp vegetable oil

1) Boil shirataki.

2) Sauté several slices of beef in the skillet until color changes.

3) Arrange vegetables in skillet.

**Cooking broth:**

2 Tbsps sugar
1/4 cup sake
1/4 cup mirin
1/2 cup soy sauce
1/2 cup water

**For dipping:**

6 eggs, broken separately into individual dipping bowls

*Method*

1. Cut the beef into 6–inch (15–cm) lengths.

2. Place shirataki (or Chinese vermicelli) in boiling water for 1 minute, drain and cut into roughly 3–inch (7½–cm) lengths. Drain a second time in a colander.

3. Mix ingredients for cooking broth. Arrange meat, vegetables, tofu and shirataki attractively on a platter.

4. Place an electric skillet or gas burner with a cast–iron skillet on the table. Lightly grease with suet or vegetable oil, and sauté several slices of beef. When the meat changes color, pour 1/2 cup cooking broth over it, then add equal amounts of tofu and each vegetable (begin with white sections of Chinese cabbage first) without mixing ingredients. When the ingredients are cooked, each person serves him– or herself out of the skillet with chopsticks, dipping the food into raw beaten egg (this cools the hot food and adds flavor) before eating with accompanying rice and salad. Add more meat, tofu, vegetables and broth to the skillet as needed, keeping broth about 1/2 inch (1½ cm) deep.

## Okra and Turnip Salad

*Sweeter and tenderer than daikon, turnips are well–suited for salads. Okra is very nutritious, although not everyone enjoys its gluey texture. With its attractive star–shaped interior, it really should be on our table more often. The dressing used here is also delightful on seafood salads.*

***Ingredients: (6 servings)***

6 okra, boiled for half a minute in lightly salted water, drained and sliced thin
6 turnips, peeled and sliced thin
4 red radishes, sliced thin
a generous pinch of salt

**Basic Japanese Dressing:**

1 Tbsp sugar
1/3 tsp salt
1 Tbsp soy sauce
3 Tbsps rice vinegar or slightly diluted cider vinegar
1 Tbsp dashi or water

**Garnish:**

1–inch (2½–cm) lemon rind squares, cut into fine strips

*Method*

1. Sprinkle salt on the sliced turnips, and let stand 10 minutes. Rinse off salt and pat dry.

2. Toss all salad ingredients together with dressing. Garnish with lemon rind strips.

## Rice with Parsley

*A simple, classic mainstay–wholesome and delicious.*

***Ingredients: (6 servings)***

3 cups short grain rice (see page 14 "How to cook rice")

3 Tbsps chopped fresh parsley

*Method*

Cook the rice and serve in individual rice bowls garnished with chopped parsley.

## Green Tea Bavarian Cream 

*The richness of cream is paired with the refreshing flavor of green tea powder. Used in the Japanese tea ceremony, green tea powder infuses this classic dessert with a glowing light green color and haunting flavor.*

***Ingredients: (6–cup long–stemmed serving bowl)***

2½ Tbsps (20 g) gelatin powder

1/2 cup (120 ml) water (to moisten gelatin powder)

2 Tbsps green tea powder (*matcha*)

6 Tbsps (90 ml) hot tap water (to dissolve green tea powder)

3 beaten egg yolks

1/2 cup (120 g) sugar

2 cups (480 ml) milk

1 cup (240 ml) whipping cream

**Garnish:**

1/3 cup (80 ml) whipping cream for decorating

1 Tbsp sugar

*Method*

1. Dissolve gelatin powder in measured water.

2. Add 1 tsp from the measured sugar to the green tea powder. To this gradually add measured hot water, stirring with a small whisk to make a smooth paste. Strain with a fine sieve to remove any lumps. Reserve.

3. Beat the remaining sugar gradually into beaten egg yolks. Heat milk to lukewarm, then gradually add to the egg yolk mixture. Heat in a double boiler or a pan over low heat, stirring until the mixture thickens slightly. Slowly add dissolved gelatin and green tea powder until completely blended.

4. Whip 1 cup of cream until its consistency is like that of the egg mixture, then mix the two well. After moistening the inside of a large serving bowl, pour in the entire mixture. Chill in the refrigerator until set (2–2½ hours).

5. For garnishing, whip the additional 1/3 cup of cream, adding sugar, until stiff. Just before serving, generously pipe out whipped cream onto the surface of the Bavarian cream, using a pastry tube. Serve cold.

# Sushi Extravaganza

*Although most people think of sushi as rice crowned with raw fish, there are actually many varieties of this typically Japanese dish. If you have access to a good fish store, you'll want to try hand–wrapped sushi, one of the most gorgeous and simplest varieties (your friends can have fun assembling their own at the table). A light, clear soup and a low–calorie traditional Japanese dessert round out this sushi party menu.*

**Japanese–Style Chicken Soup**
**Hand–Wrapped Sushi**
**Gelatin Crystals and Fruit with Syrup**

## Japanese–Style Chicken Soup 

*A pretty–to–look–at, nutritious broth of chicken and vegetables.*

### *Ingredients (6 servings)*

7 oz (200 g) boneless chicken breast or thigh, skin and fat removed
3 oz (85 g) carrot, sliced thin
12 snow pea pods, strings removed
salt (for boiling snow peas)
cornstarch (for coating chicken)

**Seasoning for chicken:**

1 tsp sake
a generous pinch of salt

**Broth:**

6 cups dashi (see page 36)
1 tsp salt
1½ tsps soy sauce

**Garnish:**

Six 1/3–inch (1–cm) lemon rind squares

### *Method*

1. Cut the chicken in 1–inch (2½–cm) thin squares, cutting at an angle. Season with sake and salt, and let stand for 10 minutes. Lightly pat dry.

2. Cook the snow pea pods in lightly salted boiling water for 2–3 minutes. Drain and cool quickly under cold running water.

3. Coat the chicken pieces lightly with cornstarch so that they retain their shapes during cooking. Cook in lightly boiling water for 2–3 minutes or until done. Drain and put aside.

4. If desired, cut the carrot slices into flower shapes using a cookie cutter. Cook the carrot in dashi until soft. Add salt and soy sauce. Place equal amounts of chicken pieces and 2 snow pea pods into each serving bowl, then pour in hot broth. Top with lemon rind squares, and serve immediately.

# **Hand–Wrapped Sushi** *(Temaki–zushi)*

*Although there are many possible filling combinations, it might be best to try the suggestions at the end of the recipe first before your inspirations. For your guests who don't like raw fish, roast beef or smoked salmon can be a tasty filling. Children will like sliced ham or omelette rounds. For diners hesitant to eat seaweed, nori can be replaced with romaine lettuce. Just be sure that each seafood or omelette filling is wrapped along with a vegetable.*

## ***Ingredients (6–8 servings)***

Sushi rice: See page 41 "How to cook sushi rice."

**Fillings:**

*Cut into 2 × 1/3–inch (5 × 1–cm) slices*

3½ oz (100 g) tuna, fresh or frozen for sashimi

3½ oz (100 g) snapper and/or flounder fillet for sashimi

3½ oz (100 g) cleaned and skinned squid for sashimi

six 6 × 1½–inch (14 × 4–cm) slices smoked salmon, cut into halves crosswise and rolled to the same size as other cut ingredients

1–2 Tbsps pickled capers (bottled) as a condiment for smoked salmon

3½ oz (100 g) salted salmon roe

2 pieces tarako (salted cod roe sac)

several dashes of sake to make cod roe paste

3½ oz (100 g) crab meat, canned or parboiled (if unavailable, substitute 3 sticks imitation crab meat, cut in halves lengthwise)

20 green shiso leaves (if unavailable, 2 or 3 romaine lettuce leaves)

1 package daikon (white radish) sprouts (if unavailable, 3 or 4 stems watercress)

2 eggs, beaten with 1 tsp sugar and a pinch of salt

vegetable oil (to grease frying pan)

12 medium–size shrimp, heads removed, deveined

1 large cucumber

**Wrapping:**

15–20 sheets nori (dried seaweed)

**Seasoning for cooking shrimp:**

2 Tbsps sake

a generous pinch of salt

**Condiments:**

2 Tbsps wasabi paste

3½ oz (100 g) ginger root

**Pickling mixture for ginger root:**

1 Tbsp sugar

3 Tbsps rice vinegar or slightly diluted cider vinegar

**Dipping sauce:**

soy sauce

## *Method*

1. Pickle the ginger root (see page 21 "Pickling ginger root") about 1 hour before mealtime.

2. Prepare the sushi rice (see page 41 "How to cook sushi rice"). Place in a large bowl with 2 or 3 large spoons for guests to serve themselves.

3. Make an omelette roll: heat a frying pan (nonstick coated is best), lightly greased with vegetable oil applied with tissue paper (this swab is used several times for greasing pan). Pour 1/3 of the beaten eggs into the pan, spreading thin and even. When the egg mixture is no longer runny, but still slightly moist, roll the egg sheet as tightly as possible from one side of the pan to the other side, forming a tube. Grease the pan lightly using the swab (even beneath the tube) and pour another 1/3 of the egg mixture into the pan, letting the new layer of egg seep under the tube as well. Roll it back to the former position, wrapping the first tube as tightly as possible, tilting the pan occasionally. Repeat this process a third (last) time with the remaining egg mixture and set firmly by wrapping omelette roll tightly with aluminum foil (or you can compress it with the kind of bamboo mat used for rolling sushi). After the omelette has cooled, unwrap and cut crosswise in little finger–size rounds.

4. Devein the shrimp, then thread a fine skewer from the top section to the tail to prevent curling when cooked. Cook in seasoning until pale pink all over, for about 2 minutes, turning occasionally. When cool enough to handle, remove skew-

ers, twisting them gently so as not to damage the shape of the shrimp, then peel.

5. Cut tips off the ends of the cod roe sac and cut in half crosswise. Squeeze out the tiny eggs from inside using the back of the cutting knife. Add several dashes of sake to the roe and make a paste.

6. Cut each sheet of nori in square quarters with a knife, and place on a plate.

7. Place all ingredients on a large platter. To create a roll, scoop about 1 tablespoon of rice and "spread" from corner to diagonally opposite corner onto a sheet of nori (shiny and smooth side against your palm), sparingly dab a bit of wasabi paste to taste, then place 2 or 3 fillings of your choice on top of rice lengthwise. Roll nori over the fillings to form a cone. Dip a bit in soy sauce before eating. No wasabi paste is necessary for omelette rounds, salmon roe and tarako. Be sparing in your use of salmon roe and tarako, as they may overpower accompanying fillings. Serve pickled ginger root as a pungent contrasting relish.

---

**The following filling combinations are "classic":**

1. Cucumber and sesame, with wasabi or mayonnaise;
with cucumber, shiso leaves or daikon sprouts
2. Tuna, snapper, flounder or squid with wasabi;
3. Shrimp with wasabi;
4. Smoked salmon with capers;
5. Tarako only or with squid and wasabi;
6. Crab shreds with omelette round or with wasabi;
7. Omelette round.

**The following are contemporary filling combinations:**

1. Avocado with wasabi;
2. Roast beef with watercress, shiso leaves or daikon sprouts;
3. Cocktail franks (prepared according to package directions) with ketchup or mustard and shiso leaves;
4. Ham and cheese alone or with shiso leaves or daikon sprouts.

1) Spread sushi rice diagonally onto a sheet of nori.

2) Place selected fillings on top of rice lengthwise.

3) Roll nori from the edge to form a cone.

# Gelatin Crystals and Fruits in Syrup
## *(Furutsu mitsumame)*

*A traditional Japanese dessert full of nostalgia for many Japanese. I call the diced, jelled agar–agar "gelatin crystals" because these glistening cubes call to mind the image of crystal glass. A low–calorie dessert with colorful fruits of the season, these "crystals" are often topped with sweet azuki bean paste or ice cream.*

### *Ingredients (6 servings)*

1 bar (about 0.28 oz / 8 g) agar–agar

2¼ cups (530 ml) water

2 Tbsps sugar

1 or 1½ cups of fresh or canned fruits, cut into bite–size pieces

1/3 cup raisins, softened in warm water for 10 minutes, then drained

**Syrup:**

1 cup (250 g) sugar

2 cups (480 ml) water

### *Method*

1. By hand, break the agar–agar into small pieces. Soak, completely immersed in a bowl of water, for 20–30 minutes.

2. Squeeze out excess water from agar–agar pieces with your hands and place in a saucepan with 2-1/4 cups water. Heat until the agar–agar has dissolved completely into gentle viscosity, laced only with soft lumps. Add the sugar. When the sugar is completely dissolved, strain to remove any remaining soft lumps.

3. Moisten the inside of a mold with water and pour in mixture, smoothing the surface with a rubber spatula. Keep in refrigerator until set (agar–agar sets at room temperature, but refrigeration speeds up the process), about 20 minutes. Unmold and cut in 1/2–inch (1½–cm) cubes.

4. For syrup, heat the water and sugar together until sugar has dissolved. Bring to room temperature, then chill in the refrigerator.

5. Mix agar–agar or gelatin cubes with fruits, raisins and syrup. Serve cold in individual cups or bowls.

1) Break the agar–agar into small pieces.

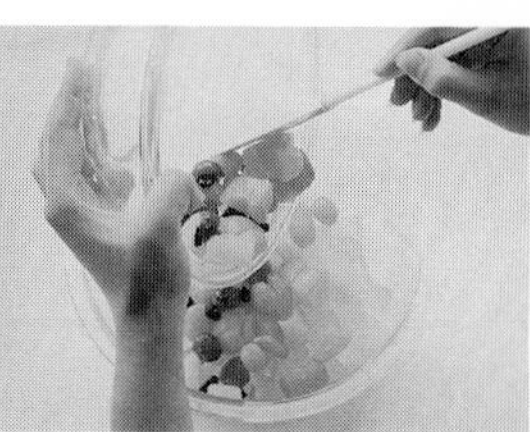
2) Mix fruit with agar–agar cubes.

# *Prepare—Ahead New Year's Brunch*

*From among the traditionally rich Japanese repertoire of 25–30 New Year's dishes, I've chosen twelve year–round recipes that appeal to the Western palate and are relatively easy to prepare. Each dish symbolizes prosperity for the new year in either name or appearance. Together they are decoratively arranged, customarily in three–tiered lacquerware containers. Every dish is "prepare-ahead," but the soup and dessert should be served hot.*

**The Top Container (Appetizers and Salads)**
Stuffed Cucumber Bamboos
Marbled Eggs
Grilled Prawns in the Shell
Marinated Daikon and Carrot
Twisted and Knotted Daikon and Carrot
**The Middle Container (Grilled and Pan–Fried Foods)**
Grilled Salmon with Teriyaki Sauce
Oriental Chicken Patties
Pinecone Squid
**The Bottom Container (Simmered Foods)**
Simmered Root Vegetables
Simmered Freeze–Dried Tofu

**New Year's Soup with Mochi**
**Sweet Chunky Bean Soup with Chestnuts**
For 6 or more servings

## The Top Container

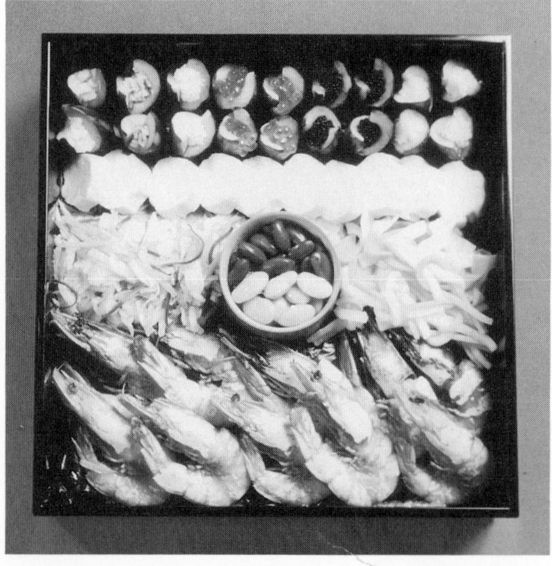

### Stuffed Cucumber Bamboos *(Wakatake kyuri)*

*These decorative cucumber chunks symbolize the bamboo often used in ornaments to celebrate the New Year.*

#### *Ingredients*

3 large Japanese cucumbers, preferably straight

**Stuffings:**

1 Tbsp salted salmon roe
1 Tbsp caviar
1 Tbsp chopped ham
1 Tbsp cream cheese
1 Tbsp cottage cheese
1 Tbsp corn, cooked in lightly salted boiling water, drained, or use canned corn

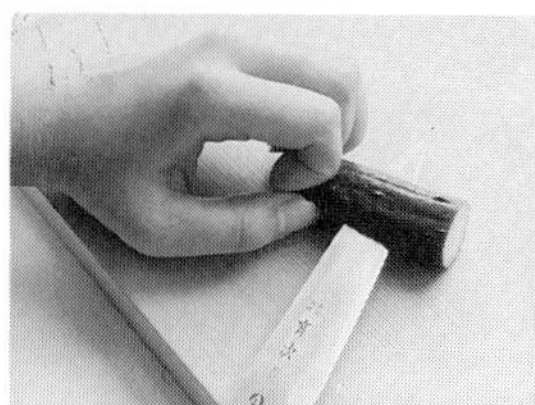
1) Cut in 2-1/2–inch (6-1/2–cm) lengths.

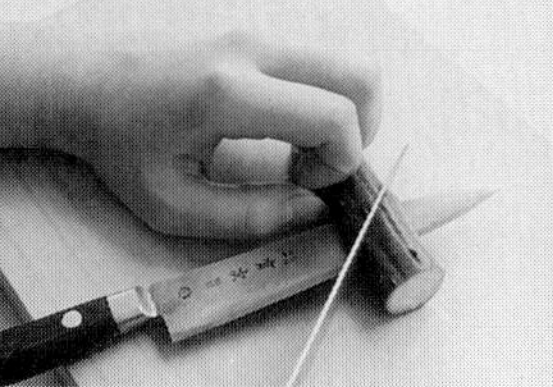
2) Diagonally cut each piece in half.

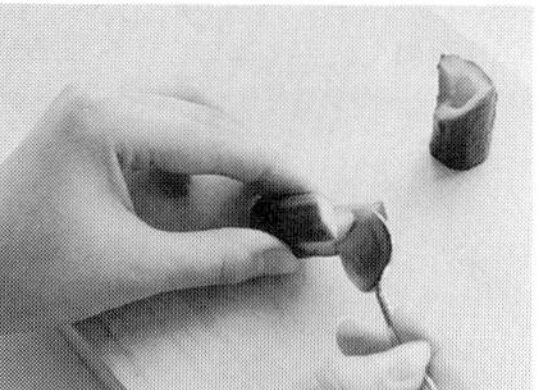
3) Make a small hollow in the center of the diagonally cut side of each piece with the tip of a teaspoon.

*Method*

1. Pare each cucumber decoratively, making vertical stripes. Cut both tips off. Cut each cucumber into 3 portions, then cut each piece in half diagonally.

2. Make a small hollow in the center of the diagonally cut side of each cucumber piece with the tip of a teaspoon. Just before serving, fill 3 cucumber pieces with a teaspoonful of each type of stuffing.

## Marbled Eggs
### *(Ganseki tamago)*

*These beautiful marble–like egg rounds will intrigue and tempt your guests.*

***Ingredients (1 roll)***

4 large hard–boiled eggs, shells removed

**Seasoning:**

1 Tbsp sake
1 Tbsp sugar

*Method*

1. From hard–boiled eggs, 4 yolks and 3 whites are used for this recipe (the leftover white can be chopped and used for salads or dressing). Remove yolks from whites of hard–boiled eggs. Mash yolks. Dissolve sugar in sake and blend with mashed yolks. Chop whites into penny–size pieces and mix with yolks. Place mixture on a damp dish towel (or aluminum foil), and roll tightly, forming a cylinder about 1½ inches (4 cms) in diameter. Fasten ends tightly with rubber bands and press firmly from both ends to make compact.

2. Place wrapped egg mixture in a steamer and steam over high heat for 7–8 minutes. Cool to body temperature and unwrap gently. Cut in 1/2–inch (1½–cm) thick rounds.

1) Chop egg whites into penny-size pieces.

2) Mix together chopped egg whites and mashed yolks.

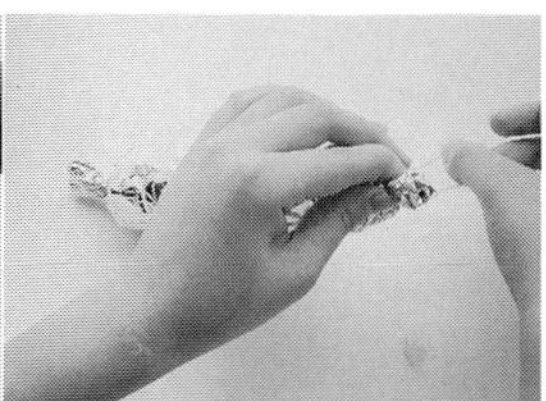
3) Form a cylinder using aluminum foil or a damp dish towel.

## Grilled Prawns in the Shell
### *(Ebi no onigara yaki)*

*The Japanese often serve prawns, shrimp or lobsters for celebratory occasions. Served with the head still on, they make a dramatic appearance!*

***Ingredients***

12 prawns or large shrimp with heads

**Seasoning:**

3 Tbsps sake
2/3 tsp salt

*Method*

1. Cut off the tips of the feelers and legs of the prawns. Devein by inserting a toothpick between the shell segments and pulling up gently, but leave the shell on. Season with sake and salt for 15–20 minutes, turning occasionally.

2. Grill the prawns* until pinkish and lightly browned in places. Turn once and cook the other side, taking care not to overcook. Guests may remove the shells before eating.

*Japanese traditionally serve seafood with the head left, tail right and stomach side facing the diner. Since the side that faces the flame first cooks most nicely, begin by cooking the side to be turned up on the serving plate.

## Marinated Daikon and Carrot *(Namasu)*

*This and the following recipe provide rare appearances of fresh vegetables among New Year's dishes. Always prepare four times as much daikon as carrot for this* namasu.

***Ingredients***

14 oz (400 g) daikon (white radish), cut into julienne

1 medium carrot (3½ oz /100 g), cut into julienne

rind of 1/4 lemon, cut into fine strips

2–inch (5–cm) square piece dried kelp (*konbu*), wiped with a damp dish towel and cut into very fine strips with scissors

1 oz (30 g) snow pea pods, strings removed

salt

**Marinade:**

2 Tbsps sugar

1/2 cup vinegar

1/2 tsp salt

*Method*

1. Squeeze out, as tightly as possible, excess moisture from carrot and daikon strips. (If it is difficult to draw moisture from carrot, sprinkle a little salt before squeezing. Do not sprinkle salt on daikon.)

2. Combine all ingredients except snow pea pods, and soak in marinade overnight, turning occasionally.

3. Cook snow pea pods in lightly salted boiling water for 1–2 minutes. Drain and cool under cold running tap water. Cut into fine strips diagonally. Before serving, mix in snow pea strips with the marinated daikon and carrot strips.

## Twisted and Knotted Daikon and Carrot *(Tazuna daikon ninjin to Musubi daikon ninjin)*

*Tasty as well as decorative, these optional garnishes are fun to make.*

***Ingredients***

a) Twisted type:

2–inch (5 cm) long daikon (white radish) (7 oz / 200 g)

4–inch (10 cm) long carrot (7 oz / 200 g)

1/2 tsp salt

b) Knotted type:

5–inch (12½–cm) long daikon (white radish) (18 oz / 500 g)

5–inch (12½–cm) long carrot (9 oz / 250 g)

1/2 tsp salt

**Seasoning:**

2 Tbsp sugar

6 Tbsps rice vinegar or slightly diluted cider vinegar

*Method*

1. For the twisted type, cut the carrot in half crosswise, then cut six to eight 2 × 1/2–inch (5 × 1½–cm) paper–thin oblong slices lengthwise. Make a 1/2–inch (1½–cm) cut in the middle of each slice. Do the same with the daikon. (One of each carrot and daikon slices are to be combined to make double–layered twisted shapes.) Sprinkle daikon and carrot slices with measured salt to tenderize, for 4–5 minutes; rinse off salt, then pat dry.

2. Lay 1 daikon slice on each carrot slice, and take one end of both slices through the cut in the middle. Pull back end. Now you have a rein–like twist. Do the same with remaining slices of daikon and carrot. Soak in seasoning for 10–20

*Sprinkle carrot slices with salt to tenderize, for 4–5 minutes.*

minutes. Drain lightly and store in refrigerator until ready to serve.

3. For the knotted type, cut the carrot in 5 × 1/6–inch (12 × 0.5–cm) fine strips. Cut the daikon the same way. Sprinkle both with measured salt to tenderize, for 4–5 minutes; rinse off salt and pat dry.

4. Take 1 strip each carrot and daikon and, together, tie a simple knot in the middle. Do the same with remaining strips. Soak in seasoning (the same used for the twisted pieces) for 10–20 minutes. Drain lightly and store in refrigerator until ready to serve.

## The Middle Container

### Grilled Salmon with Teriyaki Sauce
### *(Sake no teriyaki)* 

*This recipe's popular teriyaki sauce can be used for tuna and swordfish as well as meat.*

***Ingredients***

6 fillets salmon

**Teriyaki sauce:**

1 Tbsp sugar
2 Tbsps sake
2 Tbsps mirin
5 Tbsps soy sauce

*Method*

1. Remove any bones from the salmon. If the fillets are longer than 6 inches (15 cms), cut in half. Marinate in teriyaki sauce for 20–30 minutes, turning occasionally. Drain and reserve the sauce.

2. Grill salmon, skin side first, on a preheated grill over medium heat until lightly browned, for 2–3 minutes each side, brushing several times with teriyaki sauce. Although the fillets are usually served hot, for this menu serve at room temperature.
Note: In place of grilling, salmon can be sautéed in a preheated and lightly greased frying pan. Pour in teriyaki sauce after both sides of the salmon are almost cooked, then continue cooking for another 1–2 minutes.

### Oriental Chicken Patties
### *(Noshidori)* 

*Wonderful for parties, these patties have been one of the most popular dishes in my cooking classes. Although I've used fan–shaped patties here, one of several traditional Japanese shapes, you can create any appealing form.*

***Ingredients***

1¾ lbs (800 g) finely ground lean chicken
1 beaten egg
1 Tbsp sake
1 Tbsp sugar
2 tsps fresh ginger juice (grate ginger root and squeeze out juice)
2½ Tbsps soy sauce
vegetable oil for sautéing

**Toppings:**

1/3 cup green nori powder (if unavailable, use finely minced parsley)
1/3–1/2 cup toasted white sesame seeds or poppy seeds

*Method*

1. Combine all ingredients and mix to a pasty

consistency with your hands. Divide into 2 portions.

2. Into a preheated and lightly greased frying pan, press with a spatula 1 portion of the meat mixture to 1/2–inch (1½–cm) even thickness. Cook over medium–low heat, pricking the surface here and there with a fine skewer or fork to speed cooking, until the underside of the meat has become lightly browned. Turn over and immediately sprinkle the exposed surface with green nori powder, covering it completely. Continue cooking the other side until brown. Remove from the pan and cool to room temperature.

3. Do the same with the second portion of chicken paste, but this time, in place of nori powder, sprinkle the surface with toasted sesame or poppy seeds.

4. Cut and form the patties into "folded fan–shaped" pieces: Form a large square 6 × 6 inches (15 × 15 cm) from each patty and cut in three even portions. Cut each portion into 6–8 trapezoidal pieces like the design of a backgammon board or "folded fans" (cut at a diagonal, making alternately long and short ends).

5. Pierce each piece lengthwise through the shorter end with a bamboo skewer.

## Pinecone Squid
### *(Matsukasaika)*

*These pretty pinecone shapes are also perfect for serving at Christmas time. The pinecone's pine tree is evergreen, symbolizing longevity.*

***Ingredients***

10½ oz (300 g) cleaned and skinned squid

**Seasoning:**

| |
|---|
| 1 Tbsp sugar |
| 1 Tbsp mirin |
| 2 Tbsps soy sauce |

*Method*

1. Finely score the surface of the squid with a knife held at an angle, to avoid cutting through. Score again at right angles, but this time cut through the squid in roughly 2–inch (5–cm) squares as you go. You should have a fine grid pattern on each square piece.

2. Cover the squid pieces in boiling water and cook for 1 minute. This removes excess moisture and curls them, giving them the appearance of pinecones. Drain.

3. Over medium heat, simmer the seasoning in a saucepan, uncovered, for 1–2 minutes. The seasoning should become syrupy. Add squid, turning continuously for even flavoring for 1–2 minutes. Avoid overcooking, or the squid will become tough and chewy. Cool in the pan, turning occasionally for even coloring and flavoring.

# The Bottom Container

## Simmered Root Vegetables
### *(Nishime)*

*Though New Year's dishes have changed along with the times, this is one dish which has steadfastly remained pristine and unmodified. The various shapes and distinct flavors of these edible roots merge and blend in a delicately sweet, simmered broth, revealing to us once again the earth's hidden treasures.*

***Ingredients***

| |
|---|
| 3/4 lb (340 g) boneless chicken thigh or breast, skin and fat removed |
| 2 medium carrots (7 oz / 200 g), cut into 1/2–inch (1½–cm) thick rounds (for a festive look, you can form carrot pieces into flower shapes by using a cookie cutter) |
| 7 oz (200 g) burdock root, fresh or canned |
| 7 oz (200 g) lotus root, fresh or canned |
| 7 oz (200 g) bamboo shoot, boiled or canned |
| 8 dried shiitake mushrooms plus their soaking water |

4–inch (10–cm) square piece dried kelp (*konbu*) plus its soaking water
2 cakes konnyaku (yam cakes)
2 oz (50 g) snow pea pods, strings removed
2 tsps vinegar, to add to soaking water of burdock and lotus roots
1 Tbsp vegetable oil (for sautéing chicken and konnyaku pieces)
salt, for boiling snow pea pods

**Seasoning for chicken:**

2 Tbsps sake
2 Tbsps soy sauce

**Cooking broth:**

4 cups dashi (see page 36) including the soaking water from dried mushrooms and kelp
4 Tbsps sugar
2 Tbsps mirin
6–6½ Tbsps soy sauce

*Method*

1. Completely cover the dried shiitake mushrooms in roughly 2 cups lukewarm water and soak for 15–20 minutes or until soft and spongy. Squeeze out excess water, and reserve the soaking water to mix with dashi for the broth. Discard stems. Score a crisscross on each mushroom cap, if desired.

2. Soak the kelp in approximately 1½–2 cups tap water for 1–2 minutes, then cut lengthwise in 1/2–inch (1½–cm) wide strips with a knife or scissors. Tie each strip into a knot. Reserve this soaking water for the broth also.

3. Cut the chicken in 2–inch (5–cm) squares and season with sake and soy sauce for 15–20 minutes.

4. Scrape the skin off the fresh burdock root using the back of the knife. Cut diagonally into 1/3–inch (1–cm) thick slices. To prevent the root from discoloring, soak immediately, immersing in tap water with 1 tsp of vinegar for 10 minutes. Then drain and rinse off vinegar. (If you're using canned burdock root, soaking isn't necessary.)

5. Peel the lotus root and cut in 1/3–inch (1–cm) thick rounds and soak immersed in tap water with 1 tsp vinegar in the same way as for burdock root. (If you're using canned lotus root, soaking isn't necessary.)

6. Cut the bamboo shoot in 1/2–inch (1½–cm) thick rounds or half rounds.

7. Cut the konnyaku cakes in 1/3–inch (1–cm) oblong pieces crosswise and cut a 1/2–inch (1½–cm) slit lengthwise in the center of each piece. Take one end of the piece and push through the slit, pulling back (see twisted carrot on page 110). Do the same with the remaining pieces.

8. Cook the snow pea pods in lightly salted boiling water for 1–2 minutes or until tender. Drain and cool quickly under cold running water.

9. Heat a large, heavy pot, lightly greased with vegetable oil, and sauté chicken pieces until the undersides have become lightly browned. Turn and sauté the other sides, then remove pieces from the pot and set aside.

10. Sauté the konnyaku pieces in the pot for 1–2 minutes to remove excess moisture. Add dashi (containing soaking water from dried mushrooms and kelp) and sugar, and heat to dissolve sugar. Add all vegetables (including knotted kelp pieces) except snow peas, cooking over medium heat for 10 minutes, covered. Add mirin and soy sauce, and continue cooking for another 10 minutes. Return the chicken pieces to the pot and continue to cook for another 5 minutes, turning occasionally, until all ingredients have become tender and well seasoned. Arrange vegetables and chicken in the serving container and garnish with snow peas here and there.

## Simmered Freeze–Dried Tofu *(Koya–dofu)*

*Among several stories about the invention of freeze–dried tofu, one has it that a Buddhist priest accidentally left tofu out to freeze one winter day and, not wanting to waste this healthy food, came up with this dish.*

### Ingredients

5–6 pieces freeze–dried tofu (*koya–dofu*), reconstituted (follow package directions)

**Cooking broth:**

3 cups dashi (see page 36)

4 Tbsps sugar

1 Tbsp soy sauce

### *Method*

Bring the broth to a boil in a large, wide pot (great width is necessary because freeze–dried tofu swells after soaking in the hot broth, and should be cooked in one layer). Add the tofu pieces. When the undersides have absorbed the broth and swelled, turn so that the other sides swell to the same volume. Then continue cooking over medium heat, covered, for 15–20 minutes, until almost all the broth has been absorbed. Cool, drain, then cut each piece into squares. (For a decorative effect, Japanese traditionally cut diagonally at an angle to make wavy patterns, but you can, of course, cut into any appealing, manageable shapes you wish.)

## New Year's Soup with Mochi *(Zoni)*

*Always served at New Year's in Japan, baked, sticky rice cakes, or mochi, are a special part of this soup in which the other ingredients vary from region to region. In Tokyo the soup is clear, while Kyoto's has a white miso base. Mochi is made from glutinous rice, steamed and then pounded smooth into round or square shapes, eaten in place of ordinary rice.*

### Ingredients

7 oz (200 g) boneless chicken breast or fillet, skin and any fat removed

half a large carrot (3½ oz / 100 g), sliced thin

7 oz (200 g) daikon (white radish), cut crosswise into thin slices, cut into halves or quarters

6 fresh (or reconstituted dried) shiitake mushrooms, stemmed and cut into halves

12 stalks trefoil (*mitsuba*) greens, (if unavailable, use 12 snow pea pods)

1–inch (2½–cm) square piece lemon rind, cut into fine strips

6 pieces mochi (rice cakes)

**Seasoning for chicken:**

2 tsps sake

a generous pinch of salt

**Broth:**

6 cups dashi (see page 36)

1 tsp salt

2 tsps soy sauce

### *Method*

1. Cut the chicken in 1–inch (2½–cm) squares diagonally, holding the knife at an angle, and season for 10 minutes.

2. Cook the carrot and daikon in the dashi and salt for about 2 minutes, then add the chicken, continuing to cook for 2–3 minutes more, skimming the surface. Add mushrooms and soy sauce, cooking 1 minute more.

3. Cut the trefoil in 1–inch (2½–m) lengths. If you're using the snow pea pods, remove strings, then boil in lightly salted boiling water for 2–3 minutes or until tender. Drain and cool quickly under running tap water.

4. Toast the mochi until puffed, watching carefully not to burn them, and place one in each serving bowl. Pour piping hot soup with chicken and vegetables over the mochi. Serve hot garnished with trefoil and lemon rind strips.

## Sweet Chunky Bean Soup with Chestnuts
## *(Kuri zenzai)*

*A hot, thick, aromatic, sweet dessert soup more or less smooth or chunky in consistency, depending on the texture of the azuki beans after cooking. As well as chestnuts, another ingredient customarily included in this soup is mochi (not present in this version), cut into small morsels. Add a small amount of boiling water if you'd like this final course to be more soupy.*

### *Ingredients*

1½ cups (300 g) azuki beans
1⅕ cups (300 g) sugar
12–18 chestnuts, cooked and pre–sweetened (or use bottled)
a pinch of salt

### *Method*

1. Soak the azuki beans for 6–7 hours or overnight in a volume of water 3–4 times the amount of the beans.

2. Cook azuki beans in soaking water over medium heat. When the water begins to boil, add 1 cup of cold water to keep the skin of the beans from shrinking. When the water boils again, drain beans in a colander to remove bitterness. Return to the pot and add cold water 1 inch (2½ cm) higher than the beans. Simmer over low heat for about 1 hour or until beans have become soft. Scoop out excess water until beans are just covered.

3. While continuing to simmer, add sugar in thirds, each time mixing continuously until sugar has dissolved. Add a pinch of salt. Serve hot in individual bowls, each topped with 2 or 3 chestnuts.

# *Soba Noodles for Health and Long Life*

*Soba (buckwheat) noodles are eaten all year round, but especially on New Year's Eve as a wish for longevity, symbolized by the noodles' long strands. (Another symbolic connection is found in the time–honored "seeing out the old year and greeting the new," called in Japanese* toshi–koshi soba.*) Although the classic soba with tempura requires perfect timing, here I've introduced a preparable–in–advance soba menu. Meat, eggs and vegetables go into the soba toppings, balanced by a plentiful salad from the sea. A luscious cake made partly from buckwheat flour is the finale to a hearty celebration of health.*

**Soba Medley**
**Marine Salad with Vinegar–Ginger Dressing**
**Soba–Ginger Cake Roll**

# Soba Medley

*Long regarded as a health food, soba noodles have more vitamin B and protein than many other kinds of noodles. On a sweltering summer day as a great pick–me–up for lazy appetites, soba can be eaten with a chilled dipping sauce, or on a winter day, in a hot broth as a welcome respite from frosty weather. Soba noodles have a refreshing taste, going well with a wide variety of toppings and sauces.*

***Ingredients: (6 servings)***

1½ lbs (685 g) dried soba noodles

**Toppings:**

*a) Steamed chicken*
1 lb (450 g) boneless chicken breast, skin and fat removed as garnish: 2 dried red chili peppers, soaked in water for a few minutes to soften, then seeded and cut into thin rings

*Seasoning for chicken:*
2 Tbsps sake
2 Tbsps soy sauce
1/3 tsp salt

*b) Stir–fried pork*
1 lb (450 g) ground pork
1–inch piece ginger root, chopped fine
1 or 2 green onions (green parts only), sliced thin
1 tsp cornstarch, dissolved in 2 tsps water
2 tsps vegetable oil for stir–frying meat

*Seasoning for pork:*
2 Tbsps sake
1 Tbsp sugar
1 Tbsp mirin
3½ Tbsps soy sauce
1/2 cup water
2 tsps ginger juice (grate ginger root and squeeze out juice using your fingers)

*c) Paper–thin omelettes*
6 lightly beaten eggs
2 tsps sugar
1/5 tsp salt
1 Tbsp vegetable oil for frying

*d) Bean sprouts*
1 package (10 oz / 280 g) bean sprouts
1/2 of a large carrot, cut into fine strips 2–inch (5–cm) long
1/2 tsp salt to boil bean sprouts and carrot

*e)* 2 oz (60 g) alfalfa, rinsed and drained

*f)* 15–20 green shiso leaves, cut into fine strips (if unavailable, use 3–4 Tbsps chopped parsley)

**Sauces:**

*a) With flavor of soy sauce*
1 cup dashi (see page 36 "How to make dashi")
5 Tbsps mirin
5 Tbsps soy sauce
Heat together ingredients to a boil and cool.

*b) With flavor of miso*
1 cup dashi (see page 36 "How to make dash")
1 Tbsp sugar
2 Tbsps sake
3 Tbsps mirin
5 Tbsps miso, (nonsweet)
Heat together ingredients to a boil and cool.

*c) With flavor of sesame*
1 cup water
1/2 tsp granulated chicken stock or 1/2 chicken cube (bouillon)
2 Tbsps sugar
6 Tbsps soy sauce
3 Tbsps rice vinegar or slightly diluted cider vinegar
1 Tbsp sesame oil
1/4 tsp Chinese hot oil (*rayu*) or Tabasco
2 Tbsps ground sesame seeds
Prepare chicken soup: boil measured water, together with chicken stock and sugar, then cool. Stir in remaining ingredients.

**Condiments:**

2–3 Tbsps prepared wasabi
fine strips of rind from 1 lemon
1/3 cup chopped green onions
1/4 cup grated ginger

***Method***

1. Prepare toppings:

*a) Steamed chicken*

Season the chicken for 10–15 minutes, then steam in a steamer over high heat until cooked, for about 10 minutes. When cool enough to handle, tear with fingers or cut with a knife into 2–inch (5–cm) long shreds. Garnish with chili pepper rings.

*b) Stir-fried pork*
Combine seasoning ingredients for pork. In a heated frying pan with measured oil, fry chopped ginger for a moment, and add ground pork, stirring continuously. When the color has changed, add seasoning and cook 1 more minute. Mix in green onions, then stir dissolved cornstarch into mixture to thicken.

*c) Paper-thin omelettes*
Into lightly beaten eggs, stir measured sugar and salt, until dissolved. Heat a frying pan well, then grease lightly with vegetable oil using a swab or paper towel. Pour about 3 tablespoons of the egg mixture into the pan, tilting the pan to spread the layer of egg thin and even. When the underside is cooked (this will happen extremely quickly), flip over and cook the other side for only one second (if the surface is not runny or wet at all, no cooking is necessary), then transfer onto a cutting board. Repeat with the remaining egg mixture. Stack omelettes and cut into quarters, then into fine strips. (These paper-thin omelettes are also good as topping for salads or "wrapping" for sushi, instead of nori.)

*d) Bean sprouts*
Rinse bean sprouts of husks and debris. Cook 1 minute in lightly salted boiling water. Drain and cool under cold running water. Squeeze lightly to remove excess moisture. Cook the carrot strips in the same way, but boil for a good 1 minute, then drain.

2. Cook dried soba noodles: add soba noodles to 1 gallon (4 liters) or more of boiling water, stirring to keep noodles from sticking together. When the water returns to a boil, add 1/2 cup cold water to reduce the heat and to prevent the outer coat of the noodles from dissolving. Two or three more times let water come to a boil and reduce heat again with a half-cup of cold water. Follow the directions on the soba package (cooking time depends on thickness of the noodles), cooking until al dente. Drain and rinse under cold running water, tossing noodles lightly with fingers to remove any remaining starch. Drain well and mound on a platter. (Serve immediately.)

*1) When the water returns to a boil, add some cold water.*

*2) Rinse noodles under cold running water, tossing gently with fingers.*

**Note:** When cooking soba noodles use an ample amount of water. If necessary, use more than one pot.
Arrange all toppings on one or two large serving platters. Set out condiments and sauces. Provide each diner with a bowl to place a heaping mound of soba noodles. Each diner dollops a topping and a sauce over the noodles, then mixes before eating.

# Marine Salad with Vinegar-Ginger Dressing

*Besides being low in calories, sea vegetables are rich in minerals, are good sources of vitamins and also provide edible fiber, making them culinary gifts from nature. They are used here along with prawns, scallops and other vegetables in a seafood salad suitably accompanied by a piquant dressing with a hint of ginger.*

***Ingredients: (6 servings)***

6 prawns, heads and veins removed
6 shucked scallops, fresh or frozen for sashimi, sliced into 2 or 3 thin rounds

7 oz (200 g) squid, fresh for sashimi or frozen for cooking

salt for boiling frozen squid

5 oz (140 g) octopus, boiled and sliced thin

7 oz (200 g) crab meat (or 6 sticks imitation crab meat), shredded in small pieces

1/5 oz (6 g) dried or 1 oz (28 g) fresh salted wakame (sea vegetable)

1 oz (28 g) any other kind of edible sea vegetable (optional)

1 package (6 oz / 170 g) daikon (white radish) sprouts, rinsed, with roots cut off

1 Japanese cucumber, sliced diagonally into thin pieces

1 red onion, cut in half lengthwise, then sliced into thin half–rounds, soaked in water for 5 minutes and drained

1/2 medium carrot, cut into fine strips

1 stalk of celery, strings removed, cut diagonally into 1/2–inch (1–cm) wide pieces

1/2 lemon or 1 whole lime, sliced thin with peel

**Seasoning for boiling prawns:**

3 Tbsps sake

a generous pinch of salt

**Vinegar–Ginger Dressing:**

6 Tbsps (90 ml) rice vinegar or slightly diluted cider vinegar

2 Tbsps water

1 Tbsp sugar

1/2 tsp salt

2 Tbsps soy sauce

1 Tbsp fresh ginger juice (grate ginger root and squeeze out juice with your fingers)

*Method*

1. With seasoning, cook the prawns until pinkish all over (about 2 minutes), turning occasionally. When cool to handle, remove shells, but leave tails and the last section of each shells intact.

2. If you have fresh squid, cut into fine strips. If the squid needs cooking, score on the diagonal by holding a knife at an angle. On the same diagonal, cut into 1½–inch (4–cm) slices. Cook in lightly salted boiling water for 1–2 minutes or until squid pieces have curled. Drain.

3. If you're using dried wakame, soak in water for 10 minutes, and drain. Then cook in boiling water for 1 minute, drain and cut into 1–inch (1½–cm) lengths. For fresh, salted wakame, rinse off salt and soak in water for 5 minutes, then follow same directions as for dried wakame. Rinse other optional sea vegetables, drain, then cut into bite–size pieces and use as is.

4. Arrange seafood and vegetables in a large serving bowl or platter, garnished with lemon or lime slices. Combine salad dressing ingredients and serve separately, alongside the salad.

## Soba–Ginger Cake Roll

*Baking home–made cakes and cookies with buckwheat flour is still a relatively new phenomenon in Japan. Although two kinds of flour are used here, the characteristic smell of buckwheat is tempered by the addition of aromatic ginger and cinnamon. Since buckwheat absorbs more liquid than regular flour, orange juice has been added to increase moistness. Alluring butter–cream, spread between layers of cake, has an almond fragrance.*

***Ingredients: (One 8–inch [20–cm] roll)***

1/2 cup all–purpose flour

1/4 cup buckwheat flour

2/3 tsp baking powder

2/3 tsp ground ginger

1/4 tsp ground cinnamon

a pinch salt

1/2 cup (125 g) sugar

4 egg yolks

3 egg whites (save fourth egg white to be used in almond butter–cream filling)

3 Tbsps orange juice

3 Tbsps butter, melted in a double boiler

**almond butter–cream filling:**

4 oz (1½ cups / 115 g) unsalted butter or margarine, softened to room temperature

1 egg white, whipped until stiff

4 Tbsps (32 g) confectioners' sugar

6 Tbsps (35 g) ground almonds

**Garnishes:**

2 Tbsps sliced almonds
3–4 Tbsps chopped almonds

*Method*

1. Preheat the oven to 400°F (205°C). Mix together both flours, baking powder, spices and salt. Sift twice.

2. Line the bottom of a 10 × 8–inch (25 × 20 cm) jelly–roll pan with wax paper.

3. Whisk egg yolks, stirring in 2 tablespoons (30 g) sugar out of the measured sugar until creamy.

4. Whip the 3 egg whites until stiff, stirring in the remaining sugar (6 tablespoons, 95 g) by thirds. Fold in egg yolk mixture, then by thirds the flour mixture. Stir in orange juice followed by melted butter.

5. Pour the mixture into the prepared pan, smoothing an even surface. Bake for 8–10 minutes or until the cake is well risen and golden.

6. For almond butter–cream filling, cream measured butter: beat butter (or margarine) until soft. Whip 1 egg white, stirring in confectioners' sugar by thirds, then fold into the butter mixture. Stir in ground almonds and mix until smooth. Put aside 1 heaping tablespoon of the butter–cream to spread on the outside of the cake roll later.

7. Turn the baked cake over onto foil or dish towel. Moisten the wax paper lining lightly with water (use a wet brush), then peel off gently. Trim any crusty edges with a knife. Parallel to the short side, beginning 1 inch (2½ cm) from the edge, score 4–5 very shallow slits (1/2 inch apart). This will avert any cracking and make it easier to roll. Spread the surface of the cake with almond butter–cream filling, slightly thicker at the end with scored slits, and put no filling within 1/2 inch (1½ cm) of the other end. Roll up the cake from the side with the thick filling, gently peeling away the foil or towel to be used for support as you go. Chill in the refrigerator, seam–side facing down, until the almond butter–cream filling has set (30 min.).

8. Spread the seam–side half of the roll with remaining almond butter–cream. Sprinkle with garnish of chopped almonds. If the almond butter–cream doesn't spread easily, warm briefly in a double boiler. With the seam–side facing down, garnish the top with 2 lines of sliced almonds. Cut the roll into 1–inch (2½–cm) thick round slices before serving.

**Acorn squash** ***(Kabocha)***
Actually a variety of pumpkin, the Japanese *kabocha* used in this book is similar to the American acorn squash. *Kabocha* have dark green skins, but can be eaten unpeeled.

**Agar–agar** ***(Kanten)***
A jellying agent extracted from a sea vegetable, agar–agar usually comes freeze dried, in stick, powder and flake form. It congeals at a much higher temperature than Western gelatin, and thus does not soften or get runny at room temperature.

**Azuki beans** ***(Azuki)***
Azuki are small red beans that are usually boiled and sweetened and then mashed into a paste or used as is for Japanese desserts. The smooth paste with the skin of the beans strained out is called *koshi–an*, while the paste including bits of unmashed azuki beans is called *tsubushi–an*.

**Bamboo shoots** ***(Takenoko)***
The young shoots of bamboo are dug up in spring, so they are only available fresh during season. The rest of the year they can be found water–packed or canned. Cut whole shoots in half, then rinse off any grainy white residue before cutting into smaller pieces. The shoots may be used in a variety of dishes, including stock–based dishes, salads and soups. Once a container is opened, the shoots will keep for 5 to 6 days refrigerated in a sealed container, filled with water that is changed daily.

**Bonito flakes** ***(Katsuo–bushi)***
*Katsuo–bushi* are shavings from the fillet of steamed and dried bonito, which, along with dried kelp (*konbu*), are a principal ingredient in Japanese soup stock. They are also tasty additions to tofu and rice (just sprinkle and add a bit of soy sauce and grated fresh ginger). If refrigerated in a sealed plastic bag, they will last for 2 to 3 months.

**Cellophane noodles** ***(Harusame)***
Cellophane noodles are white, dried filaments made from the bean or potato starch (those made from beans are firmer in texture than those made from potato). Steep in hot water for 10–15 minutes, or boil 3 to 4 minutes, and drain. After rinsing in cold running water, cut into smaller lengths and use in salads, soups and sautéed dishes.

**Chili peppers**
These chili peppers are frequently used in marinades, dipping sauces and as a garnish. The seeds are very hot and are usually removed. Soak dried chilis in water before removing seeds with a chopstick. A mixture of ground red chili pepper and 6 other spices, known as *shichimi togarashi*, or seven pepper spice, is a classic Japanese condiment.

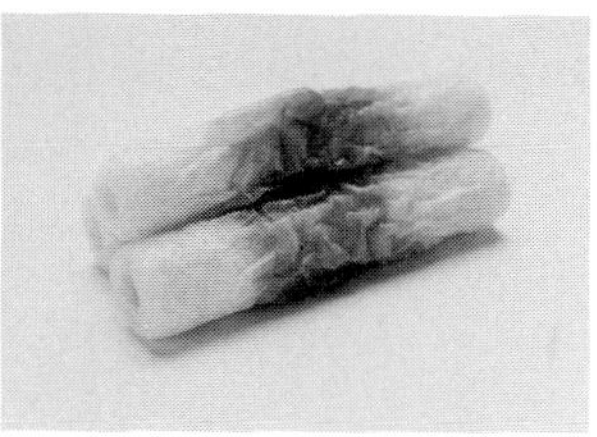

***Chikuwa*** **(Steamed fish cake)**
Made mainly of puréed white fish such as cod, *chikuwa* also contains flour, starch, *yama–imo* (a type of yam) and egg white added to make a paste. This is then made into a cylindrical shape, hollow in the center. Select ones that are resilient to the touch, as this indicates a higher content of fish. *Chikuwa* is delicious simmered with vegetables and meat, sautéed, deep–fried and as is in salads and soups.

**Daikon (White radish)**
A versatile vegetable, select firm and shiny radishes with unscarred skins. Because daikon contain a special enzyme, it is sometimes eaten grated as an aid to digestion. Appearing often as a condiment or mixed into dipping sauces, it can also be used sliced in salads, simmered dishes and miso soup, or pickled. Stored in the refrigerator, leaves removed, wrapped in damp newspaper and plastic wrap, it will keep for approximately 2 weeks.

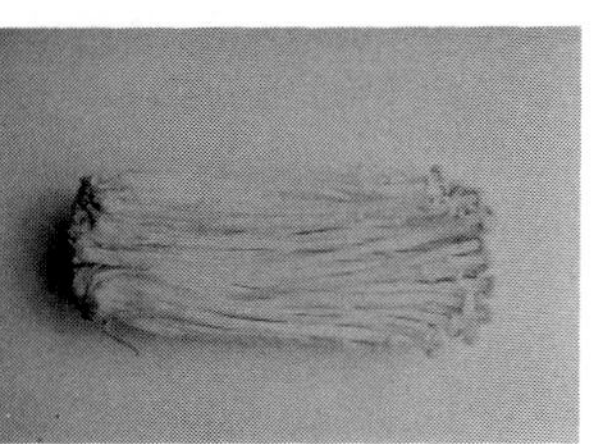

**Enokidake mushrooms** ***(Enoki*** **or** ***Enokidake)***
Also known as snowpuffs, these deli-

cate, milk-colored mushrooms have long slender stems and tiny caps. Use ones that are white and crisp (if the roots have a yellowish color, they are old.) *Enoki* should be cooked briefly (10–20 seconds).

**Freeze-dried Tofu** ***(Koya-dofu*** **or** ***Kori-dofu)***
Frozen, then dried, this type of tofu contains much protein. It can be reconstituted by soaking in lukewarm water until it swells to 1½ times its original volume, then rinsing and squeezing out excess moisture before cooking. Another, simpler method calls for using the freeze-dried tofu as is.

**Ginger root** ***(Shoga)***
Use fresh ginger, not ginger powder, in Japanese cooking. You can tell when this knobby root is fresh by its firm, unwrinkled skin. Peel and grate or mince only the portion you need and wrap the remainder in plastic and keep in the refrigerator or freezer. Helpful in counteracting the strong odor of fish and meat, ginger root is a basic ingredient in Japanese sautéed dishes.

**Ginkgo nuts** ***(Ginnan)***
These mildly sweet, aromatic nuts are sold in their shells or vacuum-packed or canned, with the shells and outer brown skins removed. Crack the shells with a hard instrument and blanch for 2 to 3 minutes in hot water before removing the skin. (Pre-shelled nuts can be used as is.) An essential ingredient in Japanese egg custard (*chawan-mushi*), ginkgo nuts are also popular in one-pot dishes and in yakitori.

**Gourd strips, dried** ***(Kanpyo)***
These shaved, dried strips of gourd are cooked in broth to absorb flavor. Select

pale white strips, avoiding old yellow, wrinkled ones. Moisten the gourd strips, sprinkle with salt and rub well to soften. Rinse and boil until soft before using. They're a standard ingredient in rolled sushi.

**Green onion** ***(Naganegi*** **or** ***negi)***
These long green onions are similar in appearance to leeks. The white part is usually eaten in one-pot dishes such as sukiyaki, in noodles and stews, and is used to counteract the strong smell of meat and fish and add flavor. The green leaves are often discarded. If *naganegi* is unavailable, substitute with scallions.

**Green tea powder** ***(Matcha)***
*Matcha* is used mainly in the Japanese tea ceremony. This powder contains vitamin C, even after adding boiling water. The fragrant, slightly bitter taste is popular for its refreshening properties. Add the hot water (let boiling water sit 3 to 4 minutes before using) to the powder, blend, and drink as is, or use as a coloring and flavoring ingredient in baking.

**Kelp, dried** ***(Konbu)***
Thick, flat, dried sheets of kelp, along with bonito flakes, are one of the two main ingredients in Japanese soup stock. The white, powder found on the sheets adds to the good flavor of kelp, and so should not be washed off (wipe with a damp cloth instead). When using, cut into small pieces or make several crosswise incisions to release the flavor.

**Konnyaku (Yam cake)**
This product is made from the yamlike root of a plant called devil's tongue, pulverized and formed into a gelatinous cake. Refrigerate in water, changing the water every day or two, and konnyaku will keep from 1 to 2 weeks.

**Lotus root** ***(Hasu*** **or** ***renkon)***
Fresh roots should have a smooth, creamy white surface with clean, tubular hollows. To prepare, first peel lotus root, then cut into rounds. Soak for a short time in vinegared water before using to prevent discoloration.

**Mirin (Sweet rice wine for cooking)**
This sweet, amber-colored liquid is made from rice and distilled alcohol. Mirin produces a pleasing flavor and sheen in cooking, most commonly noticed in teriyaki sauce. Because its use helps firm the flesh of fish and meat, it is often added at the end when simmering dishes. When a large quantity is used, as in dipping sauces and dressings, cook briefly to evaporate the alcohol before adding other cooking ingredients for a milder taste. Sake sweetened with sugar (3:1 ratio by volume) can be substituted when mirin is unavailable.

**Miso (Fermented soybean paste)**
Miso is a paste made of boiled and fermented soybeans. Its color ranges from creamy white (sweet) to light brown (nonsweet) to dark brown (salty). Although rich in protein, it should be used in moderation because of its relatively high salt content. (Usually the lighter-colored misos have a lower salt content.) Besides its use as an essential ingredient in miso soup, miso is popularly used in simmered and sautéed dishes, and in dipping sauces and dressings. Although miso will keep in the refrigerator for 3 to 4 months, it will begin to lcse flavor and aroma if kept longer.

**Mochi (Rice cake)**
Mochi is glutinous rice, steamed, mashed and formed into round or square cakes. An average commercially packaged cake of 1/3–inch (1 cm) thickness is equivalent to one bowl of rice. Although vacuum–packed mochi has a long shelflife, fresh mochi will only keep for about a week in the refrigerator. Toast or broil slowly until the cake becomes soft and puffy, being careful not to burn it.

**Nori (Dried black seaweed)**
These paper–thin sheets of dried seaweed should have a dark color and bright sheen. Toasted nori (sold as *yaki nori*, or "roasted seaweed," or made at home), the type used in this book, is crispy and has a greenish black color. Probably best known as the wrapping for many varieties of sushi, nori can also be crushed or cut into fine strips and used as a garnish. Store in an airtight container, preferably with a moisture–packet of desiccant (often included with the seaweed).

**Plums, pickled *(Umeboshi)***
These salt–cured plums come in their natural orange color, or red when pickled with red shiso (perilla) leaves. They have long been considered a health food, aiding digestion. The acidity of *Umeboshi* is helpful in preserving some foods. *Umeboshi* are often used as fillings in rice balls (*onigiri*), allowing them to be made a day ahead. Cooked with fish, they reduce any strong fishy odor and help the dish keep longer.

**Rice Vinegar *(Komezu)***
This Japanese vinegar, milder than most Western vinegars, is suitable for seasoning sushi rice and as an ingredient in dressings and sauces. (Use diluted cider vinegar as a substitute.) Rice vinegar has many healthy properties, such as stimulating the appetite and acting as a tonic in soothing stomach ailments, and also helps some foods to keep longer. It can be used to take the bitterness out of burdock and lotus roots, and to prevent discoloration.

**Sake (Rice wine)**
Sake is an important ingredient in Japanese cooking as well as a national drink. Substitute a dry white wine if sake is unavailable. Sake imparts flavor, helping other seasonings to be absorbed, counteracts strong odors and tenderizes meat and fish. The alcohol usually evaporates during cooking. Sake deteriorates fairly quickly after opening, so buy smaller bottles and use within 1 to 2 months. It is best to store sake in the refrigerator.

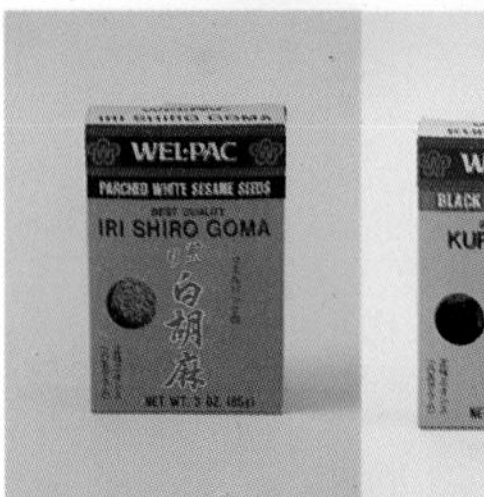


**Sesame seeds *(Goma)***
These nutritious white or black seeds are often used in dressings and sauces, and as garnish. To bring out their taste and aroma, toast them first. To further bring out their aroma (and make them easier to digest) grind using a mortar and pestle.

**Shiitake mushrooms, fresh or dried *(Shiitake)***
Good–quality mushrooms should have full, fleshy caps and a white underside. Fresh mushrooms are grilled, simmered, sautéed, deep–fried and used as an important ingredient in one–pot dishes. Dried mushrooms are more flavorful than the fresh variety and can be substituted in every case except for deep–frying.

**Shimeji mushrooms *(Shimeji)***
Shimeji mushrooms come in bunches, so to use, first cut away part of the thick bottom root, then separate into smaller clusters. These mushrooms come in light brown or gray varieties, but the light brown varieties are considered more delicious.

**Shirataki (Yam threads)**
Made of the same ingredient as konnyaku, these gelatinous noodlelike fila

ments are an essential ingredient in sukiyaki, and an important part of other one–pot dishes. Because they are low in calories and high in good edible fiber, they are often recommended for those on a diet. Look for them sealed in plastic packs (in the refrigerator section) or in cans on the shelf.

**Soba noodles *(Soba)*, Soba flour *(Sobako)***
Soba noodles are made with a combination of buckwheat flour and light wheat flour, and sometimes with *yama–imo* (a type of yam). Dried, fresh and pre-cooked varieties are available. If using fresh soba, boil for about 3 to 4 minutes until cooked but still chewy. Refer to page 119 for cooking directions for dried soba.

**Soy sauce *(Shoyu)***
Soy sauce is a traditional Japanese, all–purpose seasoning made from soy beans, wheat and salt with a harmonious balance of color, taste and aroma. It comes in regular (*koikuchi*), low salt (*gen–en*) and light–colored (*usukuchi*). Regular soy sauce is the standard type sold in supermarkets, suitable for most dishes. *Gen–en shoyu*, the milder tasting soy sauce, has less than half the sodium of regular soy sauce, making it popular with those concerned with salt intake. Light–colored soy sauce is a bit saltier than the regular variety, and is suited for use in clear soups and for aesthetic reasons in obtaining light–colored, simmered foods. Unopened soy sauce will last 1 to 1½ years. Once opened, it should be stored in a cool place and used quickly, since its color will darken and flavor weaken with the passage of time. When used in simmered dishes, soy sauce should be added after the sugar and sake have had time to cook and flavor ingredients.

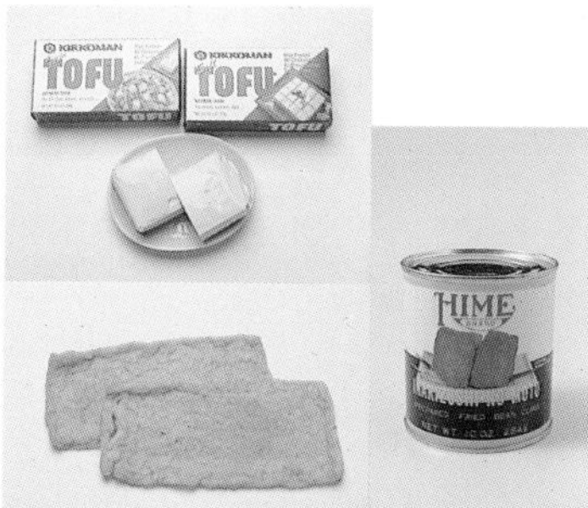


**Tofu *(Bean curd)* and Deep–fried tofu pouches *(Abura–age)***
Celebrated as a health food, tofu is economical, easily digestible, and high in protein and calcium. Its mild taste combines well with other ingredients. Firm or "cotton" tofu (*momen tofu*) is suitable for simmering and sautéing, in deep–fying and in one–pot dishes. Soft, or "silken" tofu (*kinu–goshi tofu*) is best for soups and eating uncooked. After purchasing, immerse tofu in water and refrigerate in a tightly–closed container. Change the water often. Kept in this way, the tofu will keep for 2 to 3 days, but use as quickly as possible for the best flavor. Deep–fried tofu pouches (*abura–age*) are made from tofu sliced thin and drained of excess moisture before being deep–fried. They will keep in the refrigerator for 4 to 5 days. Before using in miso soup, simmered dishes, sautéed or with sushi rice, always rinse deep–fried tofu pouches with boiling water to remove excess oil. They are available canned, labeled "prepared fried bean curd," ready to use for stuffed sushi (*inari–zushi*).

**Trefoil greens *(Mitsuba)***
This cultivated, light–green colored herb imparts a wonderful aroma to soups and stock–based dishes. Since a second of heat is all that is required to release the aroma, add to soups just before serving.

**Wakame (Sea vegetable)**
Along with kelp (*konbu*), wakame, dark green in color and smooth in texture, is also rich in minerals and fiber. Wakame

is available in fresh or dried form. To prepare fresh wakame, wash away salt and soak in cool water for 5 to 6 minutes, allowing leaves to expand 5 to 6 times their original volume. Dried wakame can be reconstituted in water (it expands to 10 times its original volume). In either case, a little goes a long way.

**Wasabi (Japanese green horseradish)**
An indispensable condiment for sashimi and sushi, freshly grated wasabi root is ideal, although wasabi paste in tubes, or reconstituted from powder is acceptable. To prepare wasabi from powder, add a few drops of lukewarm water to a small amount of powder in a small dish or cup and make a paste. Turn the cup upside down and let sit for 5 minutes before serving. Wasabi paste in a tube will last 3 to 4 months in the refrigerator. Powdered wasabi will last twice as long, although once reconstituted it should be used the same day, since the sharpness and fragrance of the wasabi will disappear quickly. Wasabi is also a popular ingredient in dressings and dipping sauces.

**Taro *(Sato–imo)***
*Sato–imo* is a taro root with brown, fuzzy skin and white flesh. Once peeled, it should be boiled for 1 to 2 minutes in lightly salted or vinegared water before draining and rinsing off remaining slipperiness. Simmer alone or with other root vegetables, or use in soup.

# INDEX